The Art of College Teaching

The Art of College Teaching

28 Takes

Edited by
Marilyn Kallet and April Morgan

The University of Tennessee Press • Knoxville

All illustrations by Jerry Weintz. They are reproduced by courtesy of
Jerry Weintz.

The art of college teaching : twenty-eight takes / edited by Marilyn
Kallet, April Morgan.-- 1st ed.
     p. cm.
  Includes index.
  ISBN 1-57233-328-6 (hardcover)
  1. College teaching. I. Kallet, Marilyn, 1946- II. Morgan, April L.
  LB2331.A649 2005
  378.1'2--dc22
                              2004022785

To our mothers, first and most enduring teachers
Diana Morgan and Cecelia Zimmerman

The teacher functions as signpost, traffic cop, Pied Piper, Zen master, or collie dog, all in the effort to move students in a particular direction. But the journey belongs to the pupil.

—*Dorothy Wallace,*
"The Hornet's Opinion"

Contents

II. Stances and Strategies: Teaching as a Balancing Act

Contents

III. Contexts: Teaching and Culture

Contents

Preface

I once participated in an interdisciplinary panel titled "Excellence in Teaching." This annual roundtable discussion at the University of Tennessee promotes dialogue between professors and graduate students in order to help prepare first-timers who are about to be thrown into the deep end. The audience was divided as to what they wanted to discuss. Some of the new teachers were worried about committing embarrassing physical gaffes, while others were more anxious about appearing ignorant in front of their students. Since I had been a graduate student when my Stupid Teacher's Moment happened (see "The Co-Creative Classroom") and mine was a mix of both classic fears, I wanted to break in and assure them, "Yes! It will happen—no matter how carefully you prepare. So don't worry that it might, don't put a lot of energy into defending against the possibility; know that it will come, and when it does, do the best you can to handle it appropriately and then get on with it."

As I listened to the other professors on the stage addressing the audience's fears and questions about down-to-earth issues like grading (do you believe in giving extra credit?), handling difficult students (do you have the legal right to kick a student out of class?), and what to include in a syllabus (is it a contract or a compass?), I was impressed with the practical teaching tips offered. For my own benefit, I started scribbling on the program pamphlet so that I wouldn't forget anything—first in the margins and eventually, when I ran out of room, on top of the program's text. Later, as I looked over my notes, it occurred to me that it might be helpful to compile accumulated wisdom—and gentle debates—into a book we could put in the hands of graduate teaching assistants for them to consult whenever they wanted a little perspective or bolstering.

After hearing Dr. Marilyn Kallet speak on this panel, I approached her with the idea to join forces on *The Art of College Teaching*. As one of our contributors says, what we've come up with is not a book of rules on how to teach well but, instead, essays that discuss some things that have worked for the authors.

With only a handful of professors on the panel, we began reaching out to others—first within the university community and later to academics across the United States. Taken together, their essays describe what one author calls "teaching syndromes" that affect us all, whether we are working at small community colleges, Ivy League research institutions, or other schools of advanced learning. Many of these teaching syndromes will probably affect all teachers, no matter how good they are. Some of the classics include wrestling with boundaries; compensating for the effects of age on teaching; struggling with diversity issues, insensitivity, and bad manners; and knowing when to stop trying to improve your students.

We are fortunate that, in addition to our local and national stars, internationally renowned experts such as champion ice-skating teacher Robert Unger and celebrated golf pro Michael Hebron who teach at the postsecondary level in their fields were willing to contribute essays. We give special thanks to artist Jerry Weintz for his spectacular illustrations because they capture the magic of it all.

April Morgan

Acknowledgments

We thank the many people who helped us to assemble this collection. Most notable among this group are our patient contributors. These dedicated teachers are also highly accomplished scholars and thus some of the busiest people on the planet. It would have been easy for them to pass on this project. We're glad they didn't. The Carnegie Foundation for the Advancement of Teaching and the Council for the Advancement and Support of Education helped us identify many of our essayists. Thank you, Cheryl M. Wesley (CASE). Dr. Jan Allen (assistant dean, the Graduate School, University of Tennessee; associate dean, the Graduate School, Northwestern University) coordinated the seminar for graduate teaching assistants where the idea for this book was sparked. We were honored by the University of Tennessee National Alumni Association's recognition of our teaching. The Graduate Studies program in English made it possible for us to have the help of a research assistant who also became a contributor, Mr. James "Bucky" Carter. George Roupe and Heather Miriam Gross expertly copyedited the manuscript. Scot Danforth (UT Press) and Joyce Harrison (formerly of UT Press) were consistent in their support for this project. Stefanie Johnson gave us an honest opinion when asked for it, and Xiaoyang Hou typed several essays. Jerry Weintz was a joy to work with; his renderings delight us. Most of all, we thank our students for forgiving us our flubs, making us want to do better, and showing us how to get there. We're working on it.

Some of these essays have been previously published. Grateful acknowledgment is made to the authors and to the editors of the publications where these first appeared for permission to reprint.

Vernon Burton, "A Special Kind of Community," Furman Magazine (spring 2001): 16–19.

Robert Langs, "Boundaries and Frames: Non-Transference in Teaching," *AWP Newsletter* 22, no. 1 (September 1989): 1–8.

Roy Rosenzweig, "Interview with Orville Vernon Burton," *History Teacher* 35, no. 2 (February 2002): 2–15; and History Matters (http://historymatters.gmu), a project of the American Social History Project/Center for Media and Learning (City University of New York, Graduate Center) and the Center for History and New Media (George Mason University).

Jane Tompkins, "We Are Educators of Whole Human Beings," Chronicle of Higher Education 43, no. 15 (1996); and *A Life in School* by Jane Tompkins, copyright 1996 by Jane Tompkins. Reprinted by permission of Perseus Books PLC, a member of Perseus Books, L.L.C.

Introduction

The Art of College Teaching began as a conversation among award-winning professors in diverse fields about issues, methods, and problems in our undergraduate classrooms at the University of Tennessee.[1] After we presented brief commentaries on our teaching—often speaking about teachers who had influenced us—the audience of new teaching assistants plied us with questions. By narrating both positive and negative teaching experiences and being listened to as if we possessed expertise, we felt valued. Our interdisciplinary, intergenerational exchange demonstrated collaborative learning about teaching. We did not want our lively dialogue to end.

Professor Morgan suggested that she and I should gather the day's discussions into a handbook for use by new teachers as well as by experienced teachers seeking to be reinspired about the profession. The project soon grew to include essays on effective teaching by professors from a variety of colleges and universities, recent winners of national teaching awards.[2] Our professors come from a diversity of community colleges and four-year universities. Some teach workshops, and others offer huge lecture classes. Their subject matter ranges from creative writing to costume design, statistical analysis to professional golf. As one might expect, their concerns vary according to their disciplines; audience and class size affect their views as well.

Those teachers who chose to write for our project offer narratives and "practitioner lore" rather than theoretical treatises. They hold in common a love for teaching, which many experience as a "calling" rather than just another day at the office. It seems that skillful teachers like to talk about teaching and to hear from those outside their disciplines. Probably most of these professors would agree with author and educator bell hooks, who asserts that teaching is a "performative act": "Teachers are not performers in the traditional sense of the word in that our work is not meant to be a spectacle. Yet it is meant to serve as a catalyst that calls everyone to become more and more engaged, to become active participants in learning."[3] However, some of our professors actually employ props and theatrics to increase active participation in the classroom.

Recent pedagogical research in teaching ecology reinforces bell hooks's belief that active learners learn most effectively.[4] Here "active learning" means that students are taught to articulate and to question what they are learning while in the midst of acquiring knowledge. This practice of metacognition can be applied to diverse fields. Many of the professors included here have long been involved in creating active learners through active teaching; they ask themselves questions about what they do and how to do it better as they are engaged in teaching.

In her essay "Teaching Writing: A Collage," Professor Libby Falk Jones shapes a portrait of process, providing memories and poems that are verbal holograms of her life as a teacher. She mentions three rhetoric/composition strategies articulated by Stephen North, from which she derives her own teaching practice: expressivist, cognitivist, and social-constructivist.[5] Like Professor Jones, the majority of our professors place high value on the process of learning rather than solely on the students' acquisition of information.

The three strategies for teaching writing that Professor Jones credits might also help us to think about pedagogy, especially if we use them to suggest approaches rather than as ironclad categories. Those professors of literature and writing whose work we have included in "We Are Educators of Whole Human Beings," place value on self-expression, self-discovery, and spontaneity in the classroom. And for their part, teachers of athletics are particularly clear and specific when talking about cognition, about how their students learn. They have derived their strategies empirically, observing how the body and the mind can be trained as one instrument to achieve mastery. These coaches are no less creative in their thinking about teaching than the writing teachers; the trainers' observations about learning carry over to other subjects and fields.

Our second section, "Stances and Strategies," gleans insights as to how teachers dramatize their subjects, as well as how they order information in order to best convey it. Dorothy Wallace, a renowned educator and professor of mathematics, delights us in "The Hornet's Opinion" with vivid metaphorical language and philosophical questions, reminding us again that creativity is by no means solely the domain of poets.

Section 3, "Contexts," continues discussion of expression, methods, strategies, and stances, but emphasizes identity and socially-derived meanings as ways of informing our teaching. Throughout these essays, we find overlapping pedagogical strategies. Our award-winning professors are inventive scavengers when it comes to pulling together the best techniques, props, activities, in order to enhance student learning.

In the opening section, "We Are Educators of Whole Human Beings," the connector is tone—we hear a respectful, affectionate attitude toward students. The professors view them as more than intellectual novices who merely seek specific information. Our professors enter the classroom ready to connect with their students, to engage intellect, emotion, and the senses in the service of learning. These professors communicate expressively, with passion for their subjects. They are willing to take risks in their teaching, to admit mistakes and move on. If vulnerability makes us clownish at times ("The Co-Creative Classroom"), so be it.

Cathleen Kennedy's essay, "Ten Surprises about Teaching," offers a model of witty, succinct thinking about teaching and being educated. Dr. Kennedy shows a willingness to hold her own preconceptions to the light, to rethink her strategies, and to ditch them in favor of more effective ones, as necessary. Her essay offers a model of "active learning" on the teacher's part. Since active learning dramatically enhances students' grasp of subject matter,[6] why not turn this method to account with respect to our own effectiveness? Dr. Kennedy uses a pop culture format, the top ten list, to engage our attention; instead of jokes, the author composes her list of misconceptions-turned-to-insights. Her encapsulated narrative about professional growth offers hope to the rest of us; her playful, yet serious quest for a dialogue about good teaching sets the tone for our volume.

Marcus Ambrester's essay, "Taste the Toads Again," argues for restoring to the classroom a sense of wonder and play. He looks back to his three-year-old daughter for cues as to how to restore the "taste" of surprise and discovery to adult learning. At the heart of his essay is anger that so much of university learning has been turned to dust by corporate thinking and uninspired teaching. Like Ken Macrorie in his revolutionary volume *Uptaught*,[7] Professor Ambrester wants to unsettle us, to refire our enthusiasm for waking up our students and ourselves to the thrills of learning, to the surprising details of everyday life that can revitalize our thinking and writing.

From the vibrant detail to the larger issue of how we live, well-known educator Dr. Jane Tompkins, whose essay gives this section its title, reflects on how to integrate the inwardness of the "cloister" (the humanities-oriented university) with the practical and ethical demands of the world: "Inside the classroom, it's one kind of student that dominates; outside, it's another. Qualities besides critical thinking can come to light: generosity, steadfastness, determination, practical competence, humor, ingenuity, imagination." While Dr. Tompkins does not answer the question of how to combine philosophical inquiry with practical skills and ethical behavior, she does show us how to value the question.

Dr. Tompkins admires the quality of humor outside of the classroom; most of our award-winning teachers also call upon humor every day at work. Throughout our volume, Jerry Weintz's cartoons remind us not to take ourselves too seriously. We teachers would be "dead sharks" or dead ducks without our sense of play. As if to underscore these notes about humor in the classroom, my daughter Heather, a music major at Northwestern University, just called with a story. Today was the first day of her internship with the Chicago All-City High School Band. She was delighted by the bandleader, William Johnson, music director for the Chicago public schools. "He smiled the whole time," Heather reported. "At one point, all of the lights went out onstage. He fixed the problem and came back still smiling. Then he said, 'The only thing I can control is my smile!'" After only a few hours of observing Mr. Johnson, my daughter had for the first time become interested in teaching as a profession.

No one would argue against the idea that teachers can have an enormous impact on their students. In section 1, on holistic approaches to teaching, a refrain emerges: "Do no harm." This dictum is stated by creative writing professor Phyllis Raphael in "Teaching for Minimalists" and in my "Beyond the Three Bears." Implicit in this guideline is the sense that harm has been done, somewhere else perhaps, to students.

In fact, a former student of mine attended a prestigious writing program at a well-known university with a renowned poet as the writing professor. The young woman, a promising poet, entered the workshop with enthusiasm for writing. The professor consistently tore her work to shreds. About one of her lines he said, "If I had written a line like that, I would shoot myself in the head." My former student did succeed in earning her M.F.A. from this program, but she could not write poetry for several years after she graduated. When she finally returned to writing, she refused to show her poetry to anyone.

In practicing "no harm," we acknowledge that as teachers we have the potential to influence our students not merely in our specific subjects but throughout their lives. We engage our students as capable human beings, learners, and peers. Our students should never have to pay with their self-respect in order to gain from us what we know.

Apropos of our students' well-being, another theme in section 1 is that of boundaries—and not breaking them. In his classic essay "Boundaries and Frames," psychologist Robert Langs emphasizes the impact of teachers and argues that learning takes place effectively when psychological and physical boundaries are meticulously observed. If we agree with this premise, then how do we assimilate the message of Father Leopold Keffler in "Three Loves," who declares that he is in the habit of giving hugs to his students? Or that of Professor Michael Flachmann, who encourages teachers to become involved in our students' lives outside of class?

A careful reading of Father Leopold's essay reveals that he has modified his behavior in recent years to include unlocked doors and open curtains at home. Recent church scandals have obviously had an impact on his behavior, making him more cautious in his demonstrations of affection. Being more thoughtful about physical displays of affection does not limit his love for his students. On the contrary, this respect is a "hands-off" demonstration of caring. And we note that Professor Flachmann's extracurricular activities with students involve sports and clubs—carefully defined activities that permit him to get to know his students better within structured boundaries. He also reports his willingness to listen to their problems and then to help them find appropriate help so that their learning is not hindered by medical or social problems. By agreeing to listen, to be a mentor as well as a professor, to place learning in the context of lives, Michael Flachmann has much in common with Father Leopold.

Among the essays in this first section, we include two by noted athletic coaches, who discuss ways of integrating body and mind. Robert Unger, ice-skating coach for Olympic athletes as well as less-advanced skaters, offers detailed advice that teachers of any subject may find useful. His concern is cognition and memory, how "body memory" teaches skaters to improve. Michael Hebron's successful instruction to professional golfers has useful applications for all of us who seek not only to transmit specific skills but to engage active learning. His discussion of "stress-point learning" can be valuable to both students and professors who wish to achieve mastery of a subject. His depiction of the desired "flow state" in his students indicates not only his teaching expertise but his compassion for his students; he helps them to get past "blocks" and plateaus by offering feedback without judgment.

Our second section, "Stances and Strategies: Teaching as a Balancing Act" provides reflections on how we position ourselves with respect to the students, both literally and metaphorically. Jackie Wilcox's essay "Don't Dance with Wolves" evokes for us the importance of leadership; she writes from years of experience teaching public high school before teaching at the university. Professor Michael Keene's essay "Teaching from Behind" would seem to present an opposite view, in which the professor is more coach than sage. Yet Professor Keene's subtle professorial style is no less leadership; his "teaching from behind" shows the influence of socially critical pedagogy.

Paulo Freire's *Pedagogy of the Oppressed*[8] has inspired many of our professors to rethink their stance as authorities. Peer responses and collaborative learning methods are crucial to classrooms where the teachers view the students as co-learners, authorities, respected individuals with valued knowledge and voices. The value of collaborative learning is a theme throughout our book.

Several teachers in this section grapple with how to motivate students. One way is to integrate fieldwork and classroom study. In "The Art of Motivating Students," art historian Gayle Seymour recounts the adventures of her students as they embark on trips to view murals and then work with ninth graders to create their own enormous mural. Her students happily report that these experiences were life-changing.

Thomas Woolley, professor of statistics, reveals that he willfully loses his shyness when he lectures "on the classroom stage," where he becomes an expressive actor. Teaching is "a balancing act," according to computer scientist Dave Berque, for one must know one's subject thoroughly and also consider one's audience, often requiring the professor to juggle competing objectives, to make elegant compromises.

Rajan Mahadevan's "Teaching: Some Things That Have Worked for Me" proffers detailed notes on organizational strategies, the nuts and bolts of teaching large lecture classes in psychology. Of all our professors, Dr. Mahadevan seems to rely the least on the students' own judgment about how they are learning and what they need to learn. How much of Dr. Mahadevan's stance is influenced by sheer numbers of students? This essay provides a provocative counterpoint to some of the more peer-based collaborative learning strategies and to those teachers who view themselves as entertainers.

Nobel economist James Buchanan relies on his expertise as well as on his dynamic personality and personal authority to carry the weight of discussion in class. Yet he indicates that he also shares his research projects with his students, engaging their participation, suggesting that his teaching involves a blend of authority and community-based learning.

In "The Hornet's Opinion," Dorothy Wallace evokes for us diverse approaches to teaching, many of which we can find elsewhere in "Stances and Strategies": "The teacher functions as signpost, traffic cop, Pied Piper, Zen master, or collie dog, all in the effort to move students in a particular direction. But the journey belongs to the pupil."

In our concluding section, on contexts, identity, and culture, we note a recurrence of earlier themes—an emphasis on knowing one's subject well, on growing with the subject over time, and on maintaining a dynamic relationship to one's own approach to teaching. Graduate student James "Bucky" Carter provides helpful suggestions about classroom dynamics, about moving around the classroom as we teach. Additionally, in this section, we also discover an emphasis on cultural dynamics—specifically on how age can affect our teaching, as well as on how the race, class, and cultural identities of the teacher and students affect teaching and learning. From David Louzecky's insights gained through teaching at a correctional institution to R. D. Bucher's "Diversity-Conscious Teaching" to Vernon Burton's "Creating a Sense of Community in the Classroom," we find the accumulated insights of professors who have observed changes in the ways society views race and culture. These teachers have reinvented their strategies for waking up their students to issues of cultural identity.

Professor Linda Arthur, in her teaching of costume design, uses historical costumes as props for engaging her students in the drama of learning about past societies. We admire her strategies and those of feminist professor Helena Meyer-Knapp, whose dedication to the field of military international relations has provided her with a lifetime of challenges and insights.

Professor D. Allen Carroll's elegant address, "Good at Any Age," will be particularly inspiring to those of us who have spent decades in the classroom and wish to remain effective and fresh. For those of us who are aging, failing memory can present a challenge. Dr. Carroll offers sage advice, and his essay provides a nice balance to young Mr. Carter's essay.

Age in itself does not seem to be a predictor of political stance. Marcus Ambrester's essay, in which he identifies himself as an older teacher, embraces a revolutionary attitude toward teaching, a yearning for upheaval and reinvention of social and intellectual structures. Our only graduate student, James "Bucky" Carter, espouses a dynamic attitude toward teaching and learning, one that literally keeps him moving all day. On the other hand, Mr. Carter admits that he is trying to bend the students to his will, albeit in subtle ways, suggesting a more conservative stance than that expressed by Professor Ambrester.

No one way will serve all of us, or any of us for all time. Mr. Carter reminds us that our work is strenuous. Like athletes, we expend our physical and intellectual energies for hours, for years in the classroom. We hope we are graceful, or if we fall, that at least we will demonstrate good comic timing. As editors, April Morgan and I hope that these essays will spark strong responses in our readers and that we will hear back from you with suggestions about how to effect better teaching with strategies that have worked for you.

Marilyn Kallet

Notes

1. August 16, 2000, sponsored by the Graduate School.

2. These include eleven state and/or national winners of the Professor of the Year awards given by the Carnegie Foundation for the Advancement of Teaching in coordination with the Council for the Advancement and Support of Education over the past decade. See also the note on contributors in this volume.

3. bell hooks, *Teaching to Transgress: Education as the Practice of Freedom* (New York: Routledge, 1994).

4. Charlene D'Avanzo, "Research on Learning Potential for Improving College Ecology Teaching," *Frontiers in Ecology and the Environment* 10, no. 1 (2003): 533–40.

5. Stephen M. North, *The Making of Knowledge in Composition: Portrait of an Emerging Field* (Upper Montclair, N.J.: Boynton/Cook, 1987).

6. Andrew T. Lump and John R. Staver, "Peer Collaboration and Concept Development: Learning about Photosynthesis," *Journal of Research in Science and Teaching* 32, no. 1 (1995): 71–98, referenced in D'Avanzo, "Research on Learning," 40.

7. Ken Macrorie, *Uptaught* (1970; reprint, Rochelle Park, N.J.: Heinemann, 1996).

8. Paulo Freire, *Pedagogy of the Oppressed* (1970; reprint, New York: Continuum, 2000).

Part One

I. We Are Educators of Whole Human Beings

Ten Surprises about Teaching

Cathleen Kennedy

When I started teaching at College of San Mateo twelve years ago, I didn't know a thing about pedagogy, learning styles, or metacognition. I naïvely walked into the classroom more worried about myself and my performance in front of the class than with student learning. I just assumed learning would happen.

As I got to know my students, I found we had different ways of looking at things—we brought different expectations to the classroom. I found that many of my students didn't learn in the same ways I did, and I began questioning the way I taught.

Things didn't always work out as I had hoped. I've had my share of students sleeping in class, doing their nails, or sneaking in late on hands and knees through the back door as if invisible.

I'm still amazed at many of the things my students do—or don't do. When they're struggling with the class, why don't they talk to me about it? When I'm giving a lecture, how can they ask whether the material is going to be on the test? And when I assign homework or reading, don't they *know* it's to be done before the next class so we can discuss it together? Haven't they already been in school at least twelve years? Why don't they know how things are done?

I found an interesting description of education that I'd like to share with you. It comes from a book by James Carse called *Finite and Infinite Games:*

> There are at least two kinds of games. One could be called finite, the other infinite.
>
> A finite game is played for the purpose of winning, and the infinite game for the purpose of continuing the play.
>
> Finite players play within boundaries; infinite players play with boundaries.
>
> Surprise causes finite play to end; it is the reason for infinite play to continue.
>
> To be prepared against surprise is to be trained. To be prepared for surprise is to be educated.[1]

Far too many of our students think of education as a finite game—something to beat. As educators, we hope to instill in our students a desire to pursue knowledge for its own sake, to value their time here, and to be prepared for life's surprises.

As I think about the things that go on in my classroom, it is the things that surprise me that connect me most to my students. So, in the Letterman tradition, I share with you today my top ten surprises about teaching.

Surprise Number 10: Students don't always know what they're supposed to do—what it is to "be a student." My evidence of this is the number of students who just "show up" each day—without reading, without working, without thinking about what we're going to do next.

It's interesting to think about how teachers and students come to have different expectations about what students are supposed to do when they take a course. It seemed to me that my students thought they were supposed to come to class, most of the time, and do the minimum work required to earn whatever grade they were trying for. Some students knew they would be satisfied with a C in the course, and that translated to attending all the classes, turning in "something" for most of the assignments, and "doing their best" on the quizzes and tests. It seemed to have no relationship to learning.

Now, I *talk* about what a C means in each course. And many students are shocked to learn that my idea of a C was their idea of an A!

Students also benefit from guidance about what to do when they're in class. When I'm lecturing, my students should be listening, formulating questions, and taking notes. Have you ever had a student constantly interrupt you because they couldn't write as fast as you were talking? They may not know how to take notes, or you may be talking too continuously. And what do your students do with those notes? We could help a lot of students by simply telling them how to use their notes for studying.

I also specifically tell my students that they won't learn all they need to know just by coming to class and listening to me. But I've come to understand that many students don't know what to do on their own—they don't know how to study. Some students think listening to a lecture is studying. Others think reading is studying. Still others think memorizing is studying. What they don't seem to get is that studying has to do with intent as much as with activity.

Surprise Number 9: Students think current teachers will be like previous teachers. This is closely tied to the topic I just mentioned but with a twist, where the student has some real evidence of how a C or an A was earned in previous courses, or when students say, "But I thought that was what you wanted!" without ever having asked what you wanted.

I think many students are in the habit of thinking of teachers collectively instead of individually and make many assumptions based on their view of what "teachers" do and want.

Of course, this is natural enough. We all tend to base our expectations on past experience. But this is especially problematic for students who have had unpleasant school experiences. Their expectation is that all teachers, all schools, are unpleasant.

This may explain why students are so responsive to teachers who make it a point to show that they care about the success of individual students—because it comes as such a surprise. At its best, recognition that teachers care about students as individuals changes the way students view education. It becomes more personal.

I do tell my students that my goal is to have each and every one in the class achieve to their optimum potential. How rare it is for students to hear these words. We think they know it, but they don't.

In an analysis of several studies of student evaluations of college professors, students were found to consistently rank the following characteristics as the most important qualities of good teachers:

(1) shows respect for students

(2) cares about student learning

(3) listens to what students have to say *about teaching.*

Teaching mechanics like "is well-organized" or "is a good presenter" consistently ranked lower than the interpersonal qualities that make students feel comfortable and welcome in the classroom and faculty office.

Surprise Number 8: Boredom is more contagious than enthusiasm. I hate to feel like I'm wasting my students' time or that we are just in class to meet an attendance requirement, but some days it does feel that way. There have been plenty of times when I've had to drag myself to class without really looking forward to it. But I had *no idea* how apparent that is to students until I saw it from the student perspective. We should all be students every once in awhile, to be reminded of what students see from their side of the lectern. Off days are one thing, but joyless teaching is a disservice to our students.

I have come to the point where I feel invigorated by being in the classroom, by focusing on what my students need, and by enjoying the subject I teach. Thinking about what my students need reminds me that I'm an advocate for their commitment to the course. If I don't believe the subject is important, why should they? If I don't believe their attendance at this particular class session is essential, why should they bother to come?

5

Some of my students have told me that they work hard in my class because they can see that I work hard in the class. I was actually surprised that they noticed and was alerted to the fact that they are paying attention to things that I thought were "behind the scenes." My guess, then, is that they also notice when teachers don't work hard to prepare for class, don't show how much they love their subject, and don't seem to care about student learning. When teachers are bored, their students will be too.

Surprise Number 7: Students think teachers work at school and students work at home. My students seem to be surprised when I tell them I do as much homework as they do! When I talk about our various responsibilities in making a class "work" I remind students that we both need to work in the classroom and at home and that I see no separation of responsibility for ensuring success of the class as a whole.

Many students think only the teacher needs to prepare for class time. What I try to explain to them is that my lectures won't mean anything if they have no context for filing away the information in their memory. And, if they can't file it away, it won't be available for recall when they need it. They'll just have to try to learn it again.

I'm sure many of us have told our students to "do the reading" *before* the lecture and to come to class with questions about the reading or about the homework. Then when we ask for questions at the next class, silence reigns. We can either assume that the students understand the material and go on to something new (and risk their not learning it at all) or cover it again thoroughly just to make sure.

The latter option can seem to students like a good reason for not reading in the first place. Why read the book if the teacher is going to tell us all about it in class anyway?

Educators no longer hold the view that our students are empty vessels waiting to be filled. Now we need to convince our *students* that it is their own effort in the classroom, as well as at home, that promotes learning.

Surprise Number 6: Students are not expecting a "sage on the stage." I'm pretty sure my first big mistake, and what actually kept me away from teaching for many years, was my perception that teachers had all the answers, spoke eloquently, and were witty and inspiring. When I finally decided to try my hand at teaching, I had come around to the idea that caring a lot about interesting students in the field of programming would overcome my native fears about speaking in front of a group, but I still held on to very high expectations of teacher performance in the classroom.

That attitude actually prevented me from making meaningful connections to my students. I was so concerned about covering the material and not making any mistakes that I didn't relax very much when I was "on." My greatest fear at that time was that I wouldn't be able to answer a student question. My second greatest fear was that if I paused to answer a question I wouldn't remember where I had left off in my lecture. I've never been very good at thinking on my feet.

I'll never forget teaching my first C programming course in 1988. I was not a C programmer at the time, so to prepare for the course, I had learned enough C to work through the problems in the textbook and develop the first couple of lab assignments. The first night in class I discovered that about half of my forty-eight students had taught themselves C and had been using it to write programs for several months. They had run into problems, which inspired them to take a class where they would have access to an expert. Me!

I still remember the experience as grueling. There was no way I could bluff; I certainly didn't have the kind of answers these students needed and expected, and I started to dread coming to class. After all, how many times can you say, "Gee, that's a fascinating question, but it takes us away from what we need to concentrate on today. Why don't we discuss that after class?"

More than any other class, this one taught me how to connect with my students. I couldn't be the teacher I thought I was *supposed to be,* and instead I became the teacher *my students needed.* I realized that students needed to know the things that weren't in the book, the ambiguities of our discipline, and perhaps most important, that working in the computer industry means constantly learning. And I was able to demonstrate that quite well. Standing before them every night was an expert who didn't have all the answers. What made me an expert was that I knew how to find the answers and use them. And I could demonstrate that process to help my students develop their own strategies for studying and learning.

It turns out that I developed lasting friendships with students from this particular class, got a little better at thinking on my feet, and came to truly enjoy teaching and the give and take of the classroom. I have found that students appreciate teachers who are human, who act as role models in the discipline, and who listen and respond to student questions and concerns. I've learned that every word I say doesn't have to be a pearl of wisdom, but it does have to be relevant and honest.

Surprise Number 5: Students think mastery of a subject is roughly equivalent to memorizing the textbook. Before we roll our eyes at how off track students are, let's ask ourselves what *we* think mastery is. We might have different opinions among ourselves, and we might even answer this question differently for different classes. What is mastery in an introductory course? Is it learning the vocabulary of the field? Is it applying the concepts to real-world problems? What

7

happens in the advanced courses? More vocabulary? More problems? What changes?

A second thing we might ask is, how do our students get the impression that memorization is key? How do we develop our tests? How are they graded? Is there only one right answer? Can students defend a different interpretation of our questions, different routes to a solution? Can they use their books and notes as a resource? Or must it all be memorized?

I'm afraid that many of my students just don't know how to use their textbooks for learning except to memorize the italicized words. They're mystified about what is important. They don't know about summarizing or reflecting on a few pages at a time. They don't think about isolating new concepts and trying them out gradually; instead they feel overwhelmed by so much new information all at once.

I try to help my students focus their attention on *learning* while reading, to be able to organize the way they use their study time, and to connect new material to their current knowledge. And I have found that I can't just assume that they already know how to do this, so I spend time in class talking about it and demonstrating how to do it. I think it's vitally important for us to teach both subject matter and study skills whenever we can. If students feel less frustrated when they study, they become more confident learners and can establish a habit of learning that they can use forever.

Surprise Number 4: Learning is a social experience. I have found that my students are more engaged when I encourage a social atmosphere in the classroom. My initial concept of a classroom was what I recalled from my own experience. Students sit at desks and keep quiet, while teachers stand at the front of the classroom and lecture. It wasn't until graduate school that I recall working in groups in the classroom. The only times I recall students speaking in class were when they were called on to present a solution on the board—always a chilling experience for me.

Eventually, I discovered that students learn from being the teacher for awhile, and I tried group assignments. I called my small groups "teams" and made the assignments a little competitive to give the team members a reason to work cooperatively.

Despite my fears about unequally balanced teams, the inevitable slackers, and the nightmare of grading group work, I have had more positive feedback from my students about working in teams than on any other aspect of my classroom strategies.

I make the classroom a social environment because I want to foster a sense of a community of scholarship; I want students to believe themselves capable of surpassing me, of teaching *me* things, and I try to demystify what teachers do. I want to encourage my students to become teachers, not only in academic institutions but in their roles as parents, neighbors, and citizens as well.

Surprise Number 3: Students think classroom teachers are the most significant factor in student learning, and rank it ahead of their own study habits in importance. Last fall, I conducted a study to compare student beliefs about participating in traditional and online courses. I polled students who had experience in online courses and those who did not. The results from those two groups were comparable in their perceptions about the factors that influence student success in on-campus and online courses.

I asked them, "What do you think is the most important factor influencing your success in a course you might take on campus? How about for a course you might take on line?"

For *on-campus* courses, 63 percent of the students ranked teacher quality as the most important factor for student success. Far behind it, in second place, 17 percent of the students ranked study habits as the most important factor. For *online* courses, study habits were the most important factor, selected by 26 percent of the students. Fewer than 5 percent of the students mentioned the teacher of an online course as the most important factor for student success.

We can draw all kinds of conclusions from these findings—and ask many more questions—but my point here is that many students don't realize how important their own study habits are for their success in school.

Surprise Number 2: Students think of education as an obstacle course rather than a way of living. Did you ever get the impression that your students are taking your course in order to check something off a list? When you ask your students why they're taking your course, do they say, "It's required"? I hear it all the time, but I don't like it very much, even if it *is* a required course.

I want my students to take my course because it's going to be fun or because they've always wanted to learn it. I suppose this goes against the natural order of things, and that's really a shame. Because it is such a pleasure to get up in the morning to attend a class about something you like, something you want to do, something that adds to your life.

One thing teachers *can* do is encourage students to see how a particular class fits into life experiences, various career choices, or building community and citizenship. Think about why you teach and what you hope to accomplish by your example.

Is it your goal to assist students in appreciating this country and becoming good citizens? To put the common good before individual good? Or is it your goal to use education to promote social justice and economic mobility? To give

9

students the skills they need to empower them politically and economically? Or do you want to help students embrace the pursuit of knowledge and intellectual achievement as goals unto themselves?

By helping students understand the interrelationships among the disciplines and between liberal studies and professional training, we help them see education as a lifetime pursuit instead of a sixteen-year-long obstacle course.

Surprise Number 1: What we do as teachers affects far more than our students. It's comfortable to think that I only need to worry about what I do in my classroom, that I can focus on my discipline and teaching strategies for my students.

But I have learned a lot from my colleagues. Had they worried only about their own classes and students, I never would have had the support and encouragement I needed to keep trying: the eye-opening conversations we had about student strengths and weaknesses; the sharing of strategies that worked, or didn't; the intellectual engagement that comes from working with colleagues—faculty, staff, and administrators—who care. Care about students, care about scholarship, and care about the institution and its value to the community.

We all need to be mentors. We need to be sounding boards. And we need to be advocates for one another, for our students, and for education. Together let's commit to continuing our conversation and promoting the scholarship of teaching.

Notes

This essay was the keynote address presented at the opening session of the San Mateo County Community College District on August 17, 1999. Professor Kennedy received the 1998–99 Outstanding U.S. Community College Professor Award from the Carnegie Foundation for the Advancement of Teaching and the Council for Advancement and Support of Education while teaching at the College of San Mateo, where she was Professor of Computer and Information Science.

1. James P. Carse, *Finite and Infinite Games* (New York: Free Press, 1986).

Taste the Toads Again

Marcus L. Ambrester

What I am about to say will seem simplistic, idealistic, or childlike to many of my colleagues. If this is true, and I think it is, I hope that many come down on the side of "childlike." I am very proud to announce that after forty-five years of teaching I have returned to such a state (I don't mean senility, but it's fine if that's what you want to call it). My philosophy is based in part on a dictum by an eminent Gestalt psychologist, Frederick Perls, who posits that each of us needs to "get out of our minds and into our senses," and that "learning is discovery." Please let me illustrate with two examples. When our daughter was three years old, I happened to be watching when she found a live toad in our backyard. First, she watched it hop for what seemed a long time; then when it stopped, she poked it with her finger and watched it hop again. Finding much delight in this process, she laughed gleefully as the toad moved. Her next step was to pick up her discovery and watch as it wriggled in her hand. She pried open the mouth, looked closely at all the visible body parts, smelled the toad, and finally licked it. She then evinced a distasteful look on her face, dropping the creature back to the ground.

Speaking of toads and discovery, my college roommate (now a neurosurgeon) once told me that when he was six, a woman who lived next door kept scolding him to get out of her yard and to stay out. He complied again and again with the first part of her order, but in his six-year-old mind he vowed revenge. One evening he listened in another room as his mother told his father that this "mean" neighbor had developed a heart condition and that any shock could trigger a heart attack. The next morning, Harry was up early joyfully hunting a toad. Harry said that after searching for a while he found a nice plump toad, crammed it into his mouth, knocked on his neighbor's front door, and as she opened it, he opened his mouth and the frog jumped out. In his account, he said that she "screamed and fainted, and I thought, 'Oh, boy! I've killed her.'" Soon, Harry was disappointed by the fact that she had only fainted, and he also grew uncomfortable with the rash that developed in his mouth.

In both cases these kids were responding to their environments, using their senses, and discovering some of what they wanted to know. As parents or older siblings, we often show great joy in our child's early accomplishments. Her first word is often greeted with cries of "Eureka!" Crawling is wonderful, walking is a "miracle," talking in sentences shows signs of "genius," and on and on through the child's early years. Her accomplishments are met with demonstrations of love on our part. So the child soon learns that sensing is joyful, discovery is great, and the love she feels from these accomplishments is reaffirming of her self-love. What a wonderful universe of which to be a part. But then come comparison and competition, and our learning process is changed forever.

Our son was born in central Texas and spent his first eight years in one of the hotbeds of athletic fanaticism. At age four he was encouraged by some members of the community to participate in the summer preschool Olympics. Each day he and his friend Ben walked to track and field practice together, spent the morning, and then came home. About two weeks after the program started, I asked, "What event do you do best?" He said, "Running." Out of my own deeply embedded Alabama socialization, I blurted, "Are you beating Ben in the races?" Marcus's reply was childlike and direct, "Ben and I just run together, Dad." Thank God! For me it was like getting hit in the head with a Louisville Slugger. What joy! What freedom! What discovery! "That's great!" I said and immediately I felt extremely sad about what was soon to befall him.

"How stupid and unscientific, Ambrester," some of you are saying, and my reply is simple: "If you are thinking something of this sort, it is time for you to quit reading and toss this into your file thirteen." For the rest, I wish to return briefly to the topic of learning and competition. Getting verbally and physically loved for every discovery you make when you are young creates a sense of inner love, psychic strength, and a thirst for similar experiences. However, it is not long before we are plunged into the competitive norms of I.G.Y.S. "I've got you, stupid!" is superimposed on us by many of the situations we face in life, and this competitive attitude is introjected into our psyche very early. "Who won?" "Come on, you're not trying! You know you are better than her!" "Carlenna's girl can already read! What is wrong with you?" "I am so embarrassed that a girl beat you up. You have brought dishonor to our family!" Etc.

It would be quite naïve to argue against hierarchies, since they seem to arise out of necessity among almost all symbol-using societies. For various reasons, as the noted rhetorician Kenneth Burke states in *A Rhetoric of Motives,* "as loquacious creatures, we cling together by forming hierarchies of Mr. Bigs, Mr. Middles, and Mr. Littles." Such a system is automatically competitive, pitting individuals and groups against each other. Many would argue that a "democratic" hierarchy is the best possible system for humans, and there is much evidence to validate this hypothesis. But must the sacred needs to be curious and to learn, discover, and create be thrown into the same bin with all the other activities in a capitalistic system? I believe that we could live, learn, create, and lead happier, more fulfilled lives in an environment in which individual learning, creativity, and discovery are received with complete affirmation and love.

Most of you have observed children as they go to school on their first day. Generally, there is eagerness, joy, excitement, nervousness, and a flood of other wonderful emotions as the children take their places among all the others, ready and happy to begin their discovery (our daughter was so excited that she could not sleep). But how long does this excitement last? How long do they jump from bed and, after a hearty breakfast, rush off to this meadow of learning? A week? A month? Gradually, many children begin to dread school. They don't want to get up in the morning, they don't like to do homework, they don't like being put in "redbirds," "bluebirds," or "blackbirds," they don't like being put in competition with every other child. As Kenneth Burke points out, the result is the development of a "trained incapacity" to learn. Children soon begin a process of memorization and regurgitation. Thus convinced that they are supposed to memorize so many of these things, they soon discover that what they call learning is competitive work devoid of excitement, and they carry these beliefs throughout their school experience.

On the other hand, it would be unconscionable for me to overlook an increasingly large group of dedicated teachers who strive daily to keep that flame of discovery alive in each child. More and more young teachers are dedicated to that very cause, and yet they are immediately stymied by a system politically motivated to force these young idealists to fit into the correct pigeonholes. Hence, to satisfy the needs of the general population as well as the military-industrial complex, they are forced to teach students to pass standardized tests. These tests are then used as "proof" of learning, and every child is in competition with every other child in the state or the nation.

Now this is a system we can all be proud of. God bless America! We look out for the "well-being" and "best interests" of our children as we mold them into the roles for which they are "best suited." Many of you may remember that about thirty years ago, many colleges "got with the times" and afforded students the "right" to select the major portions of their curriculum. And guess what: most had no idea what they wanted to take. So, falling back on conventional wisdom, many professors and administrators concluded that freshman lack the maturity to determine what they want to take in college. What a revelation! After twelve years of being told what they had to take and working in a system of "trained incapacity" for learning, these "immature" students *did not know what to take!*

So what's the big deal? We have a system that works rather well, so why bother to "kick against the pricks"? Because we are first and foremost TEACHERS!

15

We must do what we can to create change in learning, at least in our courses. Why not seek as a goal to instill the sense of wonder into each of our students about our subject matter? Why not get to know *every* student in your classes, not just by name, but also personally? Make it our objective to listen to and help them further their dreams for a fulfilled life. Help them see that if their jobs are not their "callings" they stand a good chance of living a rather dreary existence. Let them know that a "calling" is much like childhood discovery. You pursue a calling because you love it, and you get out of bed every morning with the excitement of being alive. Why not rattle their cages concerning their closed-mindedness toward ideas, beliefs, and people? Why not seek to recreate that childlike sense of discovery, which can enrich their lives through history, literature, arts, science, and communication?

"Realistically, Dummy," you object to me, "this can't be done at the university because we can't afford such student-teacher ratios." Okay, let's go the final mile:

First, eliminate 95 percent of the administration (keeping only a chancellor, a financial aid officer, and deans for each college). Second, detach all athletic programs from the university except for nonscholarship programs. Third, emphasize academic and artistic programs that offer students the opportunity to compete (such as academic debate, architecture, art, creative writing, science projects, theatre, and a host of others) and publicize these with the enthusiasm we now devote to athletics. Fourth, allow no classes to exceed twenty-five students and encourage a high rate of interaction between students and faculty. Fifth, teach in nice, sparse, clean spaces with state-of-the-art equipment necessary for our discipline. Sixth, provide a clerical and maintenance staff and pay them a *living* wage. Seventh, let the faculty make all decisions (academic and financial) through representative democratic processes. Eighth, require at least six graduate hours in teaching for all teaching assistants (taught by someone who can teach). Ninth, quit converting our institutions of higher learning into trade schools. Let them be rededicated to teaching the whole person about rediscovering herself, rediscovering the joys of learning, of writing creatively without fear of undue criticism, of communication, and of creating an environment of ontological parity. Let them discover excitement in scientific, statistical, and mathematical inquiry and experience the value and wonder of past and present civilizations, as well as the aesthetic experiences available in all the arts.

In his insightful book *The Politics of Experience,* R. D. Laing avows, "If I could turn you on, if I could drive you out of your wretched minds, I would try." Laing's statement has inspired my own statement to my students: "If I can lead you back to your childlike senses of discovery, if I can create a moment so overwhelming that you will want to participate in that moment, forgetting about time and space; if I can invite you to smell or taste the toads again and feel wonderful about the experience, and I can help you to rediscover that sense of joy in curiosity and search and run along with you to show my love and complete affirmation in your quest, then and *only* then am I teaching."

Teaching for Minimalists

Phyllis Raphael

The first book I ever read about teaching creative writing was an essay collection by writers who taught their art—*Writers as Teachers, Teachers as Writers.* Among the contributors was the short story writer Grace Paley, who advised getting students to write the truth. "Like you," she said with a dash of irony, "I was improved upon by interested persons." Among the lies she wanted removed were "the lie of writing to an editor's or a teacher's taste," and "the lie of the brilliant sentence you love the most."

The year was 1978 and *Writers as Teachers, Teachers as Writers*, published in 1970, was one of the very few books about teaching writing I could find. The book was included in the small publishing list of *Teachers and Writers*, a group funded by the New York State Council on the Arts and the National Endowment for the Arts that sent poets and writers to work with children in the public schools. I was thrilled to locate it. I was fairly desperate for information. I'd just been offered a teaching job. I wanted the job (for all sorts of reasons, some admirable, some less so), but I was clueless about what to do once I got into a classroom. I wasn't a product of a writing program, nor were most writers I knew in those years. I was self-taught, but what I had taught myself I couldn't tell myself, much less a class.

The man who invited me to teach was of very little help. In fact, we'd met when I'd come to ask *him* to help me. Dick was a novelist who taught in a tiny writing program that hung like an afterthought at the tail end of a college English department. The university that housed the department had established an M.F.A. program in writing in a proper "School of the Arts," but Dick had refused to join it. Instead he'd hung on in the college English department where he'd been for years, accepting as students all sorts of gifted but nonmatriculated writers from the world of New York as well as the university. Several years after I'd begun writing and publishing, I'd registered for one of his classes to find out what I had been doing and how to continue doing it. There was a sixty-year-old postmaster from Georgia in my class who'd just published his first story collection and a woman writing a novel about the death in adolescence of her mentally impaired younger brother. She couldn't read it aloud, so someone had to do it for her while she turned away from the class, silently weeping.

After a couple of semesters in Dick's writing workshop—during which I'd managed to keep writing without learning how—he'd offered me this job. Not only did I not know how to write, I didn't know how to teach, either. I was about to embark on a two-career swindle, with the power and prestige of an eminent university backing the scam.

I called Dick and asked if he'd at least give me some teaching pointers. He said, "Ah . . . OK" and met me for lunch (late) at a Chinese restaurant. Dick was from Michigan and had a homey, folksy, midwestern way about him. He punctuated his speech with a lot of *ah*s and chuckles. "Ah . . . don't be modest. You know what to do. Don't do too much. There's not much you *can* do anyway." I thought he was going to stop right there, but instead he told me a story. He said that when he was an impoverished student at the University of Michigan he'd been able to earn twenty-five dollars every two months by giving blood. But the twenty-five bucks barely got him through a month. Since he'd won a few prizes in college short story contests, one day when he was downtown in Ann Arbor and noticed a little magazine office he went upstairs and asked the editor if he could write for him. The editor showed him a short story by Irwin Shaw. "Can you give me something like this?" he asked. Dick took the story back to his dorm, read it ("I thought it was a pretty good model"), and that night wrote one of his own and returned with it to Ann Arbor the next morning. The editor said, "Not bad," and cut him a check for a hundred dollars. "This was better than giving blood!" He wrote another and then another. After a couple of hundred-dollar checks he began to think, "There could be some money in this writing business" (chuckle). Maybe he could make a killing with bigger magazines, say, the *Saturday Evening Post* or *Look*. Before he sent those places anything, though, he thought he'd better collect some more information. He was, after all, about to hit the majors. So he went to the library, read everything he could find about the art and craft of fiction writing, and at the end of six weeks of research sat down and wrote a story and sent it off to the *Saturday Evening Post*. Two weeks later they sent it back. So did *Look*. And *Ladies Home Companion*. And ten other national magazines. Finally, figuring a hundred dollars was better than nothing, he brought the story down to the little magazine office in Ann Arbor, where the editor also rejected it. "What happened to your writing?" the editor asked. "Oh God!" he moaned when Dick told him what he'd done. (Dick said he actually remembered him slapping his palm to his head.) "It will take you years to get over that."

"Don't learn too much," Dick said. "It will only get in your way."

I gave it one last shot. "Can you give me *any* other suggestions?" I asked. After a couple of seconds he managed to come up with something. "Don't hurt anyone," he said.

We finished our chow mein, said good-bye, and Dick, a handsome, white-haired man with striking blue eyes and a beard, ambled up Broadway. He wore a heavy white turtleneck sweater hand-knit in Santa Fe, where I'd heard he'd literally built his own house. He looked like the perfect writer, as if central casting had sent him up for the role. His writing students swore by him, and like all great teachers, he had rumor and mystique swirling about him. It was said that one of his novels had been edited by Maxwell Perkins, Thomas Wolfe's legendary editor. Dick could get away with saying nothing, I thought. He could get away with anything. All he had to do was stroll into a classroom and sit down. He never had to say a word.

A dozen students came to my first workshop on a snowy January night. I was replacing Dick that semester, and I thought all of them would bolt when they saw not him but me. But miraculously only one guy clumped out—his wet boots leaving a trail of water from his seat to the door. By then I'd made a decision to take the advice I'd collected; what choice did I have? To me that meant getting my students to write a lot and write quickly. I'd learned from my own work that the more you write, the less you think and the more likely you are to encounter something honest, something you didn't know you knew. I asked them to write lists and conversations, descriptions and events from their past. I asked them to write about their mothers and fathers, colors and losses and places. I asked them to write from points of view they didn't like or understand. Having them write a lot took care of filling up the two hours of weekly class time. We had a lot of pages to read and comment on. I also tried not to say too much. Almost anything I could think of to say might be right one time but wrong the next, right for one writer but wrong for another. Much of what I'd heard said about writing sounded clichéd and ridiculous. And most of the advice I could think of could be easily contradicted by some smart kid. Also, the less I said, the more unlikely it would be that they'd try to write to please me, and when I did finally say something, they'd listen. For each piece of writing I tried to find the one comment that wouldn't hurt; maybe it would even help, although that might be too much to hope for.

One of the students in that first class was the wife of the head of the history department. She was a good writer—easy to respond to. It would have been simple to "teach too much" about her stories with their domestic details and wifely undercurrent of resentment. But instead I just aimed to keep her appetite high so she'd keep going. The point was always to get rid of all those "interested, improving persons" Paley had warned against, to break through to the voice that told the truth. "What did he promise her in the taxi?" "How high was his fever?" "She dropped the Steuben glass! Really?" By the end of the semester I can't say that the heat of her discontent had burned through the roof of the classroom, but the sparks had begun to ignite. While it shouldn't have mattered that her husband ran into Dick at a faculty party and he reported

Phyllis Raphael

back, with his usual chuckle, "She said the class was pretty interesting!", the tiny remark worked on my imagination—as sparing comments did on my students.

Over the years I've broadened my concept of what it means to do no harm. The short stories of Chekhov I estimate could never hurt anyone, nor could those by Raymond Carver or the memoirs of Mary Karr. So I assign them to read, along with beneficent others as they occur to me. Editing, the act of sculpting away what doesn't belong and adding what does, I reckon another nonmalignant procedure. I pick up a blue pencil and encourage students to get into the habit of looking over their own work as an editor might.

Since so much of writing is self-taught, my goal still is to keep a writer writing. The student who wrote stories about sex fretted that she was going too far. In Lisa's stories her characters—stand-ins for herself and her boyfriend Charlie—made love on rooftops, in subway stairwells, in the subterranean caverns beneath academic lecture halls. They shopped for fishnet stockings and bawdy lingerie. Each time Lisa was scheduled to read her work, the class kidded her. Where next? Buckingham Palace? The moon? Others were envious, some prudishly stand offish. Inhibitions nagged her. "Do you think I write too much about sex?" she asked in a conference. She was leaning over the desk, her voice low so no one in the nearby cubicles would hear. "Don't be ridiculous!" I said. "You don't write enough about sex. Write more!" She leaned backwards and laughed, for the moment at least, she'd continue.

In the years since I began teaching, writing programs have sprouted like weeds, and dozens of books about teaching appear annually. Teaching writing is big business for universities, community centers, theaters, YMCAs, and entrepreneurial individuals. Check the shelves in Barnes & Noble or any other chain or even one of the smaller more "literary" book stores still drawing breath and you will see them, title after title, row after row, miles of books crammed with worthy advice about story structure and arcs, raising dramatic tension, creating dialogue, and how to find a dozen different images to describe autumn rain. Writers who teach have all this information available to them now although they may not need the help. They themselves may be graduates of writing programs where they learned pedagogy from the writers who taught them, many of whom are no longer simply "teachers," or "teaching artists," but "tenured professors." When I started to think about this essay, I hunted through my bookshelf for *Writers Who Teach, Teachers Who Write*. At first I couldn't find it and thought that perhaps I might have disposed of it, given it away after the apartment was painted or when shelf space was too tight. But it was there—wedged among the books I use for reference. The Grace Paley essay was much as I remembered it, but there were others I didn't recall; one in particular by the poet Denise Levertov took me back with gratitude to my own ignorance. (I'm glad to be back and hope I can remain.) "I came to see my inexperience as something of an advantage," Levertov wrote in *The Untaught Teacher.* "Even if it made things harder for me it has meant that so far at least I have brought to teaching a freshness, a quality of improvisation that I believe my students have found stimulating." She put me in mind of others who—in one way or another—have acknowledged the essential mystery at the center of creating anything truthful: a psychoanalyst I know who steers patients away from reading Freudian or Jungian theory while they are in treatment; Spencer Tracy and his old saw for actors, "Learn the lines and don't bump into the furniture." And finally, Saul Bellow, the Nobel Prize–winning novelist who may have expressed it best: "I don't know exactly how it's done," he said. "I leave it alone a good deal."

Phyllis Raphael

Beyond the Three Bears: What I Know Now

Marilyn Kallet

I have always wanted to be a teacher, at least ever since first grade, when Miss Howe taught me to how to read. The first kid in her room to learn, I read aloud *Goldilocks and the Three Bears* to our class. Miss Howe hugged me, and that hug was definitive. Miss Howe was not afraid to show approval or affection. So I associated kindness, reading, food (porridge!), and school—one irresistible gift package. Reading had become a kind of nourishment, and a healthy addiction. By fifth grade, when the hormones kicked in, I decided that in addition to becoming a teacher I also wanted to be a writer and a policewoman decoy. Luckily teaching, writing, and having a family have provided enough of a sense of adventure that I have been able to forgo the handcuffs.

After three decades of teaching, I still feel a thrill when I walk into the classroom; I experience the drama of teaching—as the students and I are involved in creating and exploring works of art together. What privilege! What excitement to read a poetry student's first "real poem" after a dozen messy starts—to find a rhythmically coherent piece of cloth in language. The students in my writing classes are composing themselves as well as their poems—remembering, inventing, making musical shapes of experiences that were otherwise chaotic, incoherent. The stakes are high.

My motto in teaching writing is "Do no harm." Respect the creative process above perfection of craft. Encourage creative play. Maintain an atmosphere of respect and good manners when discussing others' writing. Create an environment where perfection of craft is desirable, a possibility, but not a sword. Teach writers that sanity is possible for poets and that happiness is as good a subject for poems as misery. I believe in William Stafford's credo. When he told an interviewer that he wrote every day of his life, she asked him, "What happens if you experience writer's block?" Stafford replied, "Lower your standards." I believe in high standards, and that if a writer is in this for the long haul, if writing is a way of life, he or she must learn to befriend the process. I teach my students not to dread the blank page and not to let what they expect of themselves destroy them.

I want to be a great listener, so much so that the quality of attention in my classroom will draw out of each writer his or her best and deepest work, the secret stuff that my students did not know they had in them. Censorship is the enemy of poetry. My students learn that their best work takes place only in an atmosphere of permission and trust. A unique quality of listening takes place in a writing classroom; high value is placed on each student's every word.

Like the jazz musician who improvises, the creative writing teacher learns to listen with his or her whole being. Such listening involves concentration on what each student is saying, looking him or her in the eye, responding both with elegant restatement of what the student has said and, by taking the dialogue further, exploring resonances. The teacher listens with the absolute conviction that each student has something valuable to say. Often, beneath the surface of the words, the teacher hears the sorrow that will play itself out in the student's poetry. Then she will need to show tolerance, a steady hand, discretion, and compassion.

Literature creates a beautiful, formal boundary between us and our students as well as a country of imagination where the class may dwell together for a short time. Especially for the older teacher, the temptation may be toward nostalgia, toward recycling old formulations and witticisms. In order to maintain excitement about the field of study, the teacher must immerse herself again in the literature, challenge herself to find new levels of meaning in texts that she has taught before. She must learn to integrate the latest literature into the body of work that precedes it. She must let go of even the most beloved of older texts in order to add some newer ones to the mix. It is a given that the students resist the most difficult texts. The teacher must be patient and reward students when the breakthrough occurs. Keep an eye out for those breakthroughs—the moment when the eyes light up and the poems begin to find their rhythms.

For me, revitalization of my spirit often involves going to artist colonies over vacations, talking with my colleagues about their discoveries. Recently, at the Mary Anderson Center for the Arts, I met a poet/teacher from Colorado named Deanna Kerns Ludwin. In a large carry-on suitcase Deanna had carried thirty new poetry books, none of which she was willing to be parted from. She told me, apologetically, that a brush with cancer the previous summer made her feel as if she had to make up for lost time in her reading. The books in her suitcase were terrific. She lent them to me over the course of two weeks, and my own writings were inspired by many of them. In turn, I bring the new works back to my students.

A lively teacher maintains a dynamic relationship to knowledge and to the class. The students don't usually change their seating patterns after the first couple of classes. So the teacher needs to move around among the students. The teacher is more of a dancer than a stone monument. She doesn't stand still, literally or figuratively. I am appalled when I enter a classroom and the teacher's desk takes up half of the room. Unfortunately, this is the map of 90 percent of

26

the classrooms I stroll past in the humanities building. What does this say about the teacher's fear of the students or about the teacher's ego? Most of the time that desk only serves as a resting place for papers.

As a teacher, as a mother, I am proud to be a nurturer. That old connection between reading and food still holds. Recently, one of my students commented: "The first class I ever had with you formed an impression. I was hungry and you brought me food. Since then you have helped nourish my work and encouraged me to explore and thus to grow in poetic ability." These lines in Matt Gilchrist's midterm narrative evaluation of "Dreamworks" (poetry writing from dreams) have resonance for me. At first, I thought that Matt was speaking metaphorically. Upon rereading, I realized that the hunger and the food were at first literal. Matt was a member of an early evening class; I often brought snacks. By the next semester, Matt had grown to trust me as a teacher, and he was writing probing poetry from his dreams. This fall he will be entering the M.F.A. program at the University of Iowa.

My willingness to provide for the class on the most literal level helped them to learn. The "secret" here is to provide what is appropriate to the class at hand, to be generous with teaching. Snacks can be an energy boost and a sign— friends break bread together; teachers and students can do so, too, from time to time. Chocolate works wonders.

Not all classes embody sweetness and light. Problems will occur. I have learned to deal with them immediately and directly, to confront inappropriate behavior right away. If the behavior is too disruptive or threatening, I will write it up and give a letter with all of the information to the head of the department. Any teacher, no matter how great he or she may be, will have to deal with problem students at some point. It's best not to flinch and never to make it personal.

During one session of "Dreamworks," I was so impressed with the students' new poems that I told them to memorize their poems for oral presentations in the next class. However, I had not read all of the poems in the batch. At the bottom of the stack was a poem called "My Dream of Killing the Niggers." Luckily this poem caught my eye before we all left the classroom. I stopped the author before he left the room, and I said, "You can't perform this poem. It threatens others. Write something different for the next assignment." The student responded by saying, "You are the first teacher who has ever dealt with me directly. I write stuff like this for every class. The other teachers just pretend like it isn't happening." Before leaving, this student also let me know that he kept a gun in his car to protect the vehicle against "them." I wrote up the exchange and immediately reported it to the associate head of our department. This particular student remained calm and quiet throughout the rest of the semester.

27

Perhaps the most important thing I have learned in thirty years has to do with maintaining good boundaries. When I first started teaching, I was twenty-three and my students were in their teens. It was the early seventies, and historically speaking, much of America didn't have very good boundaries. We were a "touchy-feely" bunch, often stoned, always hip. No one spoke to us about boundaries or about the devastation that lack of appropriate behavior could bring. In those days, I knew much too much about the students' personal lives, and worse, they knew too much about me. Learning took place despite this messiness.

Since then, we have all learned not to touch the students or to let them touch us. Not to confide in them. Even innocent boundary-breaking will have repercussions. If I take an undergraduate class to a coffee shop or to a play, I have to be prepared for several students to "act out" by not showing up for the next class. I can predict that boundary-breaking activities will come back to haunt me. Usually, graduate students have more maturity than undergraduates in dealing with activities out of class. And strictness with regard to boundaries applies to some subjects more than to others—for example, in teaching writing poetry from dreams I have learned to maintain pristine boundaries, since the writing is more intimate, more packed with emotion than that of the standard workshops.

For our final class in "Dreamworks" last semester, I took the students out to read their poetry at a bookstore. On the first day of the next semester, one of those same students, who was enrolled in the next course with me, approached me after class and cheerfully offered me what appeared to be a packet of Kodak photographs. I stowed away the gift in my book bag. At home, when I opened the package, I found that it actually contained a baggie of marijuana. Before the next class, I discreetly handed back the packet and said, "Thanks, but I can't accept this. As the one who's doing the grading, it's inappropriate for me to take gifts." I could have gone on about the illegal nature of the gift and how it could have gotten both of us in big trouble—but since this student was a rock musician, what would have been the point? That young man has graduated, and we are still friends. I did learn my lesson, though, about not accepting mysterious packages from students.

Though we may be dedicated teachers, we have to let go of being the only ones who can inspire our students. We must encourage them to study with other teachers. We have to let them go. Through us, they learn to critique each other's work, and their own. If we're good teachers, we are always in the process of making ourselves obsolete. We are involved in helping to create other writers with whom we can have a wonderful dialogue. Right now, for example, I am

Beyond the Three Bears

involved in a poetry group that consists of three of my former students (I taught them fifteen years ago) who are now my friends and peers. Some of our students will surpass us as writers—doesn't this mean that we are first-rate teachers?

My students who have gone on to become teachers tell me that they sometimes imitate me in their classrooms. They speak about creating an open and honest atmosphere for learning; they talk about maintaining good boundaries. Recently at the Associated Writing Program conference I met a student of mine from 1974—a poet who is now a professor at an Ivy League school. We laughed together about the messiness of teacher-student interactions in the "old days"— we shuddered to think of our mistakes. But she proceeded to remind me of all that I had taught her. And then, after thirty years, she hugged me and exclaimed, "Thank you!"

Marilyn Kallet

Boundaries and Frames: Nontransference in Teaching

Robert Langs, M.D.

I write as a teacher of professional psychotherapists and lay students; I have written extensively on psychotherapy and the nature of patient-therapist communication. Much to my own surprise, and perhaps to yours as well, I have discovered that the teaching situation shares much in common with parenting, on the one hand, and with the psychotherapeutic situation on the other. Both in the classroom and in the psychotherapist's office, relationships are powered by comparable universal and individual forces and needs, whatever their ultimate differences. And each, as we will see, requires a broadly similar frame or context to protect the well-being of those involved.

With this in mind, it becomes necessary to challenge the use of the concept *transference* to define the basic psychological dynamic between student and teacher, a dynamic that exists in every such relationship regardless of the gender of those involved and regardless of whether either the student or the teacher is aware of it—a dynamic that is present unconsciously, like it—or know it—or not. Freud and his followers define transference as a constellation of *inappropriate* perceptions of—and reactions to—an authority figure: perceptions and reactions that are said to derive from childhood relationships with parental figures and are subsequently imposed upon a present-day relationship such as that with a teacher.

In place of transference, I will emphasize the role of what might be loosely called *nontransference,* or *valid unconscious perceptions* in the teaching relationship. By this I mean the existence—outside of awareness—of a sound, undistorted, and appropriate view of the authority figure, a view *selectively influenced* by the past as presented in disguised or encoded fashion. And even though—or largely because—the experience occurs outside of conscious awareness, it exerts an especially strong emotional influence. Though the constellation is unconscious, its effects are quite real. In plain language, you and I, as teachers, play a significant role in the consciously and especially the unconsciously determined reactions of our students as an inevitable aspect of our role as authority or parental-substitute figures. And this proposition holds regardless of your particular beliefs on the matter; it is an unseen law of nature.

In order to explain my position and define some of its practical implications, I would like to introduce you to the realm of unconscious communication and to the means by which it is possible to decode transformed or encoded—essentially unconscious—messages in a way that can deeply inform you as a teacher in your relationships with your students. Indeed, by using several actual vignettes, I hope to convince you that this realm of unconscious experience, never known or articulated directly, is an extraordinarily powerful factor in every teaching situation.

To complete my argument, I will show how, in the domain of deep unconscious experience, *issues of ground rules, frames, and boundaries* are overridingly important. I will offer the results of several classroom "frame exercises," which I believe convincingly demonstrate the truth of this insight for the teaching situation. That is, the means by which you create and handle the conditions of your teaching situation and relationships is the single most important context and factor in how your students experience their work with you—and how it affects them emotionally as well.

In my own work as a teacher, I have found that the well-selected example is often prototypical. With this in mind, and with the permission of all concerned, I will begin with a candid story to which I am a party.

Some months ago, I taught a class based on my book *Decoding Your Dreams* (Holt, 1988) at a local college. As the semester neared its end, several students asked to continue working with me, and I agreed to hold a series of seminars at the hospital where I did research on unconscious communication. Thus there was a shift in the basic teaching contract—alternations in the fee, to whom it was directly paid, locale, etc.

On the first day of the new class, a woman who had elected to come to the seminars walked with me to the bus stop and told me that her husband was a publicist who was interested in my work. She said that he had offered to help me make contact with the media and to develop funding for the research I am doing. I told her that I was definitely interested in her husband's offer. A few days later, he called me and we initiated discussions on how we might work together on the projects he had in mind.

Some weeks later, in one of our dream seminars, we were discussing how to decode dreams in light of emotionally powerful stimuli. I was making the point that ground-rule or boundary issues play a special role in prompting dreams, particularly when one is in a psychotherapeutic relationship. Since we were not discussing clinical cases, I used as an example of a frame break my ongoing discussions with that woman's husband. Although it seemed to me at the time (I have since learned differently) that such issues were not as significant outside the therapeutic dyad as they are within its confines, I made clear

Boundaries and Frames

that it seemed odd to me to be working with the spouse of a student. At that very moment, the woman suddenly recalled a dream of a rat devouring her father.

This dream contains an *encoded perception* of me in light of the frame issue just discussed. The image is not unrealistic or inappropriate; it is not a transference derived almost exclusively from her past, but an accurate symbolic portrayal of the truly devouring and greedy nature of my behavior in this situation—a portrayal that is secondarily influenced by her own life history.

Granted, this is frightening business. To understand a student's communication as an encoded but valid indictment of a teacher's behavior (the teacher is held responsible), rather than a distorted and unfounded or unprovoked view (the teacher is free of blame), is clearly discomforting. But if this be the truth of the situation, then let the truth be known.

A few weeks later, with the negotiations with her husband still active, but stalling (I, too, as is typically the case in these matters, was learning all too slowly and reluctantly that it would be best for everyone if I were to renounce my exploitative but well-rationalized hopes), it was this same student's turn to present in the seminar. She reported a dream about a very attractive black man whom she kept touching and wanting to take to bed. She was willing to share him with another woman who also wanted him sexually.

In freely associating to the dream (i.e., in allowing her mind to wander unencumbered with thoughts, feelings, and images evoked by the various elements of her dream), this woman candidly told us that she had recently picked up a corporate executive who had greatly flattered her by wanting to seduce her. She had nearly complied but at the last moment had changed her mind. In the course of associating to the dream, my contact with her husband appeared quite unexpectedly—again, much to the surprise of all concerned.

To anticipate the substance of my discussion, I would propose that as a teacher I had unwittingly behaved seductively toward this woman despite my conscious wish to be conscientious about classroom ground rules and boundaries. What I mean by this is that the very act of moving a student from a college classroom to one's own private setting is unconsciously experienced—quite correctly—as seductive. Beyond that, however, as if to add insult to injury, I became involved with the woman's husband in a promotional venture. This, too, is seductive, as are all departures from the ideal frame of a teaching relationship.

Indeed, by simply decoding this woman's two dreams and her few associations, it can be said in all fairness that, apart from the devouring, aggressive, and greedy qualities of my behaviors, I was, in a sense, offering myself to this student as a powerful sexual person to be admired and seduced in turn. Further, if we look at the story of her encounter with the executive and treat this, too, as

Robert Langs

an encoded perception of my behaviors—one that was lived out instead of dreamt—we can see that my frame infringements were unconsciously perceived as cavalier, sexist, exploitative, and adulterous. There was no direct awareness of any of this, but the unconscious meaning is quite powerful. The consequences of this unconscious load of meaning were nearly disastrous for my student— as witnessed by her uncharacteristic inclination to get involved with someone other than her husband.

Though many aspects of these experiences are beyond awareness and quite unconscious, the effects are very real and directly observable. What we generally do to protect ourselves from the awful truth is fail to recognize the connection between the stimulus—our frame-deviant behavior as teacher—and the response—the student's errant action (or symptom).

Please notice that it was not necessary in this discussion for me to invoke the term *transference* or to suggest the presence of distortion; instead, I am acknowledging that this woman correctly—and selectively—perceived some powerful unconscious meanings in my behavior. Oddly enough, had she been my patient, I would have expected such reactions and not become involved in the first place. In my thirty years of practice, I had never been a party to an incident of this kind. It was through this experience that I myself realized with some pain that the same principle—a need for boundaries and restraint—pertains to the student-teacher relationship as those that apply to the relationship between patient and therapist.

One other point needs to be acknowledged. Students are not always entirely unwitting victims of the teacher's frame breaks. In this instance, for example, my student prompted the contact between me and her husband. Her encoded images therefore also—though secondarily—pertain to herself, as well as to me. Nonetheless, I, as teacher, must bear the greater responsibility for this incident; neither I nor any teacher should use a student's invitation to deviate as a way of denying my own powerful role in what transpired.

We experience the world in two ways; one is direct and conscious, and the other is indirect and unconscious, known to us only through disguised (encoded or transformed) messages. In the emotional domain, *the conscious system* (conscious thinking and sorting out) is relatively inept, while *the deep unconscious system,* as I call it (unconscious reasoning as revealed in displaced messages), shows great intelligence. It is there, beyond our immediate grasp, that we process all emotionally charged information and meaning that we cannot bear in awareness. And it is there that our most painful perceptions of ourselves and others are worked over based on *unconscious perceptions.* Whenever we wish to report out the workings of this deep unconscious system, we must do so through displaced and disguised narratives and images—stories told about one group of people and in a particular setting that actually encode perceptions about an entirely different group of people and a very different setting (the two are connected by *themes* shared in common).

As we saw, my student did not dream of me directly in either of her two dreams, but of her father and of a black man. Both of these men were disguised portrayals of myself, as was her image of the rat (we are all subjected to multiple representations in our own dreams and those of others), and their attributes and actions were encoded expressions of the *implications* of what I had done.

The process I am speaking of begins with an emotionally charged stimulus or trigger that leads to a limited measure of conscious response and to an extended measure of deep unconscious reaction. These latter responses are then encoded in our stories and dreams, which can be decoded by reversing the process—by undoing the displacement and disguise, guided by the nature and implications of the triggers that set the process off in the first place. To decode, you simply lift the *themes* from the direct or surface (manifest) story and relocate them in the missing (latent) context. The surface story may be about almost anything, but the latent story will encode unconscious perceptions of our ways of structuring our relationship with the student who tells the tale.

To return again to the anecdote I alluded to a moment ago, one specific trigger for my student's dreams was my conversations with her husband. They were unconsciously perceived as adulterous, inappropriate, and seductive— among other attributes. These perceptions were then encoded in both the dream of the black man and in the patient's tryst with the corporate executive (I cannot stress enough the real consequences of unconscious perceptions). Faced with my student's dream and behavior, we can reverse the creative process and decode these images by recognizing their trigger in my contact with her husband and thereby undoing her use of displacement. In substance, we realize that the situation with the executive, for example, was used to convey perceptions about the situation with myself. It is this type of *trigger decoding* that reveals remarkable new insights into unconscious experience and the very structure of our emotional lives—and the unconsciously prescribed requisites of a student-teacher relationship.

It turns out that when we consistently apply this decoding process in light of the prevailing triggers, both the psychoanalyst and the teacher do a great deal to evoke unconscious reactions in his or her patients/students. Actually, the more we know of the *implications* of our behaviors and communications, the more we realize that the deep unconscious system is exquisitely in tune with many such implications—including those that are actually beyond our own awareness. The behavior of our students, then, is powerfully but unconsciously motivated by these perceptions as they are selectively dealt with in terms of the student's early life, emotional difficulties, and the like. If Freud had used the term unconscious *selection* rather than unconscious *distortion*, he would have been much closer to the mark. Still Freud was quite correct in one sense: there is a powerful interpersonal and unconscious dynamic between student and teacher (again, regardless of their sex), and this dynamic is influenced by the early life experience of the student (and of the teacher as well). I am simply stressing here the extent to which the teacher is accountable for the consequent behavior of the student because we typically and defensively fail to recognize many ramifications of our own inputs.

The conscious system tends to be quite cavalier and inconsistent when it comes to ground rules and boundaries, while the deep unconscious system is both exquisitely sensitive and consistent in its attitude: boundaries should be kept, frames maintained, and ground rules adhered to—no exceptions. We fight these constraints consciously because we abhor renunciation and are intensely though inappropriately gratified by deviant actions (at bottom, they help us to deny the ultimate ground rule and frame: that life is followed by and framed by death).

As I said, I have of late been carrying out frame exercises that might make for interesting creative writing classes as well. The class attempts to define the ideal frame for a particular relationship (e.g., child-parent, employer-employee, spouse-mate, student-teacher, etc.). They then present dreams or stories that come freely to mind once the frame has been tentatively delineated (or the students are asked to bring dreams and such to the next class). We can rely on the deep unconscious system to work over the frame issues and have its say through a displaced narrative, and we can expect a remarkable level of agreement among these encoded images, since we all share a fundamentally similar set of framework needs and viewpoints. Still we let the evoked imagery speak for itself, always prepared to discover something new and unforeseen. The results with respect to the framework of the teaching situation may surprise you. In the main the ideal and unconsciously sought-for teaching frame includes:

1. A fixed time and setting, with a single teacher and a consistent, unchanging group of students. This would include set office hours if need be.
2. Total privacy for the class, without observers or other intruders.
3. A measure of confidentiality, in that a student's problems are discussed privately and not in front of the class.
4. A clear set of ground rules that define requirements for attendance, grades, tests and reports, class participation, advancement, and the like.

5. A defined fee paid either to the school or, in the case of private teaching, to the instructor.

6. A clear definition of the domain of the class, its range of topics, and its rules of business, so to speak. While appropriate topics may be far reaching, extraneous topics are excluded.

7. A clear definition of the role requirements of teacher and student, without role reversal (e.g., the teacher does not explicitly ask to learn from the class but allows such benefits to occur inevitably as part of the teaching experience).

8. The student-teacher relationship and interaction is confined to the work of the class; there are no outside contacts and no other type of exchanges (e.g., of a business or sexual nature).

9. Similarly, student-student contact is restricted to the work of the class.

10. The teacher maintains relative anonymity and is not personally revealing, nor does the teacher respond to a student personally or with bias but solely in terms of the work at hand.

11. The teacher is suitably compensated and seeks no other remuneration or personal gain from the class.

12. There is no physical contact between all concerned.

These are the main ground rules; some are explicitly stated, others are implied. And even though no one among us is able or inclined to adhere to these tenets in toto, and even though there are mighty protests against their enforcement by many consciously motivated voices, it is *only* when a teacher adheres to them as closely as humanly possible (too rigid a position is usually a sign of difficulties in the teacher, even though frame breaks also signal problems as well) that a teacher is *unconsciously* experienced as having integrity, warmth, genuine concern, strength, wisdom, and the like. And of course, all too often this picture is dramatically different from conscious experience where the quest for deviations is seemingly endless despite the underlying havoc they create.

A woman teacher spoke at length to her class of another school at which she taught. During a frame exercise a woman student recalled a dream of a woman exposing her naked body at her apartment window (this, of course, is an encoded perception of the teacher's self-revelation—and an accurate one at that). A male teacher had his class to his home at holiday time. The encoded response came from a young woman who dreamt of a bald man, much like the instructor, who tried to push her into his bedroom in order to forcibly seduce her. (The repeated encoded allusions to sex and aggression are by no means a reflection of my Freudian bias but are instead an indication of the extent to which frame deviations are instinctually charged communications.)

Though all of this may run counter to your accustomed thinking, encoded images of this kind are repeated in the face of frame deviations to the point of utmost predictability. The deep unconscious system of our students asks for a strong, *inherently* supportive, "holding" relationship, which forms an ideal and neutral matrix for exploration, creativity, and growth. Frame breaks tend to be exploitative of the student or confusing and unconsciously disruptive—whatever conscious satisfactions they may afford. Once you have tuned in to the world of unconscious experience, your view of the emotional universe will change in remarkable ways. Besides, there's no cheating nature; if you depart from the ideal frame, both you and the student will pay a price, even though you are likely not to notice the cost.

On the other hand, if you maintain the ideal frame, especially in face of pressures to deviate, you will be rewarded with positive encoded images and salutary unconsciously founded responses from the student or class. Thus a teacher who used some indirect clues from his male student to turn down the student's request that he be excused from his final exam because of a recent illness was rewarded with a sensitive short story about the young man's grandfather who could be firm when needed and loving and supportive when others backed away at times of crisis. The so-called introject—the internalization of this experience—derives from the teacher's ability to hold to the ideal frame and will significantly and unconsciously support this student's creativity and character makeup. Indeed, secure frames are essential to creative teaching spaces within which a student can safely exercise and develop his or her imagination and writing skills. Deviant frames compromise these functions to some degree, though, paradoxically, a great deal of creative writing deals unconsciously with deviant frame issues—in family, school, or wherever; this helps to account for much of the creative outpouring from students who have experienced major frame alterations in their relationships with their teachers.

I will conclude my remarks with two final vignettes that I hope will help to resolve remaining resistance to these ideas. The first involves one of my friends, a woman creative writing teacher, who invited a male student from a class she taught to attend a private seminar she was conducting in her home. Her student was consciously pleased by the invitation but then began coming late to his regular class. The story he wrote after this incident involved a woman who was a thief and suspiciously seductive and who entrapped in her home innocent wayward young men new to the city. Encoded in this story was the student's unconscious perception of the teacher's well-meaning but seductive break in the teaching frame.

38

Another woman teacher called a young woman student into her office to let her know that her repeated absences would be met by a failing grade. The student explained that she was experiencing a great dread of having her work read in class, and the teacher assured her that she would not be required to do such readings if she was so terrified—there was no requisite to present in class in order to pass the course. The student was also advised to generate fiction that had a greater distance from her personal life—i.e., to use more imagination and play (remember, a well-defined classroom situation is an ideal creative and play space)—so that she would be less personally involved in her own work and better able to share it with her peers. The student's short story before this meeting had to do with a violent and psychotic mother, but the story she wrote afterwards had to do with a troubled but loving grandmother who was revered even as she was dying (this particular story was the last of the semester). Here, then, we have an instance of securing the classroom frame (the warning about lateness), and a consequent positively toned (encoded) story.

I suspect that it will be many years before we carry out indisputable research to show the powerful and sometimes devastating consequences of framework and boundary breaks between students and teachers—everything from flirtations to sexual contact to visits to the teacher's home. Many well-meaning but unconsciously destructive practices prevail in today's educational climate mainly because, first, we are deeply ignorant of unconscious experience and, second, we all share deep and abiding needs for frame breaks. Death, as I said, is the ultimate boundary for life itself, and denial of the restrictions imposed on us by rules and frames is very much a way of denying personal mortality. To some extent, psychological health requires this denial; all too often, however, the denial is overdone and leads to self-aggrandizement and abuse of others. As an added perk, most frame deviations are "wickedly" gratifying for all involved. It requires considerable character and emotional health to see and believe in the ultimate wisdom and helpful powers of the secure frame.

As a psychoanalyst and teacher who has decoded thousands of images and investigated thousands of triggers, the great majority of them frame-deviant, I can share with you a strong sense that the consequences of frame alternations are far more hurtful to all concerned than anyone imagines. The only saving grace is the discovery that human beings often react paradoxically to hurtful interventions from their therapists (and teachers) and somehow discover a means of feeling better (or being more creative) in the face of the most disruptive therapist (teacher) behaviors imaginable—though probably always with an unnoticed and hurtful price tag attached. Rarely, it must be acknowledged, the positive aspects of a truly innovative and imaginative frame break may give more to a student (and teacher) than it takes away or harms. Still we as yet have no established means of identifying these exceptions that prove the rule; until we do, it seems best to adopt a cautious attitude informed by the likelihood that all of our needs to deviate have a notable dose of our own emotional difficulties embedded in their expression.

The realm of unconscious communication is weighty. Beyond psychotherapists, those who teach creative writing have a most optimal opportunity to appreciate unconscious expressions. Indeed, on one level, every story written by a student encodes not a few telling unconscious perceptions of the work of his or her entirely new world of insight and can only enhance the teaching process and the personal development of student and teacher alike. But the disturbing side of these perceptions—the ways in which they embody virtually all perceivable aspects of our human failings and capture our own most awful communications to others—have led most of us, whether therapists or teachers, to simply avoid the decoding process. Yet those who are fortunate enough to have the strength to carry out such decoding—and the choice is not ours consciously but fundamentally based on unconscious need and capacity—can gain access to a wisdom far more consistent and telling than anything we have managed through conscious experience alone. I very much hope that this essay will stimulate more teachers to learn more about this critical domain. There is both knowledge and beauty there, for if conscious expression is the prose of human communication, unconscious expression is its poetry.

Three Loves

Father Leopold Keffler

We've all heard the standard question and its response: What are the three best things about teaching? June, July, and August. While I'm not immune to enjoying the summer, more and more I respond when people ask me, "What's the best thing about teaching?" with "Students, Students, Students." Sure, there are wonderful colleagues, and we're all glad for the break times when we can get on with the rest of our lives. In our profession, there's simply the thrill of learning things, of knowing things, of thinking and conversing, and of intellectual interchange. Still, for me, the students are the best part.

I don't know what the secret of good teaching is. I'm not sure that I would regularly line up my suggestions in the same order of importance, if asked again. Here, though, are some things I would say.

(1) Love your students. While they are in my classroom, they are my children. I teach college, but they are still my children. "My kids." I attend their games and music and theater performances and art exhibits. I feed them. I take them to the theater. I befriend them. I counsel them. I am available to them. I may not have much of a relationship with everyone in my classroom at any one time, and many of the relationships won't last for long after they have left my classroom, but the numbers mount up over the years.

Sometimes I've told a class that probably the most effective "pedagogical" device I could use to improve learning would be to give each student a hug coming into and going out of the classroom (you can see I've been influenced by Leo Buscaglia), but I'm afraid I would be looking for a new job soon if I tried that technique.

Some years ago, one of my students came to me to tell me his grandfather was dying and he needed to take a few days to be there. I could see he was deeply affected. So we talked. I asked a few questions. The grandfather had done much of the raising of him. Of course I said, "Go. That's where you need to be." Then I asked, "Do you need a hug?" He certainly did. And unashamedly grabbed hold of me right there for a while. And cried for a while. We have been close friends ever since.

Other students have recognized this therapy sometimes, too. One gave me a button a few years ago that I still wear on my habit which says: "Free hugs. No expiration date." Some students seeing that have asked, "Is that true?" And there have been hugs because of that.

It is good therapy. It is useful. It is probably also risky. And I try to judge in each case, "Is it worth the risk?" Most of the time, I decide affirmatively.

I've also taken to "adopting" some of the kids. The main consequence of this is that they are invited to my "Papa Feeds" nights. (A few in the past have asked me, "How do I get in on this?" So, of course, they are "in" right then. That's gutsy to ask a teacher for something like that.)

Once a month they are invited to be at my apartment by six, and once the group has gathered we take a vote about where we will eat that night. Usually we dine at one of the nearby buffets. It raises eyebrows and questions when I arrive and say, "Eight (or two, or ten) adults and one senior please." "Are they all your family?" In a way, yes.

They are indeed in some way "my family." They are welcome at my apartment at any time. During the summer while I am away "parish sitting," usually one or two will live there. They water my plants and my garden. They can call maintenance if there are problems. The campus security knows they are there and keeps an eye out for them. I provide housing for those who need it. Even more, this arrangement provides me with "artificial" family. And with some who entered my life as much as ten and fifteen years ago, we are indeed still family. I adopt them. They adopt me. About the first one with whom I made this arrangement, I say: "He needed a father. I needed a son. So we adopted each other."

Loving my students does, however, present this issue: How do I go about being loving, being the teacher who wears the "Free hugs" button, being "Papa Leo" to the kids who feel comfortable calling me that, and at the same time neither damage anyone (them or me) nor risk the integrity, effectiveness, or reputation of the profession?

In the context of so much current news and scandal about clerical sexual misbehavior, any affection can be misunderstood. I know that on some occasions this concern over appearances and appropriateness has inhibited my behavior. On some occasions other faculty members have raised eyebrows. And I find that some kids are embarrassed at being hugged in public, so I try to remember which ones and not embarrass them. Often, I feel angry at myself later for allowing a certain "prudence" to prevent spontaneous appropriate responses.

To deflect any suspicions, I deliberately try to maintain a certain openness or transparency. Simply keeping my apartment curtains and blinds open almost all the time (all the windows and the sliding door open onto a parking lot and path where many students pass by at all hours of the day and night) is, I suppose, symbolically saying, "I have nothing to hide."

My apartment door won't lock—it hasn't for years. Everyone knows that anyone could just walk in at any time. And some of my kids do just that. For a few minutes. For a few hours. Even to "crash" for a while. I feel really good that they feel that comfortably "at home" to do that. Not getting the lock fixed is another symbolic gesture showing I have nothing to hide.

(2) Love teaching. I love a captive audience. I love recounting stories. I love conveying thoughts and information.

I tell the students they don't stand a chance against me. I'm the oldest child in a family of three. I'm a priest. And I'm a school teacher. So I'm used to being bossy and being right and being listened to. I also grew up with a schoolteacher mother and a well-read father and a highly competitive sister and brother. Sometimes I say I spent a long time filling my head with knowledge and information. To ease the pressure, now I have this compulsion to spew it out and to share it with others.

Less facetiously, I also have this unshakeable notion that it is a sacred and important function in society to hand on the wisdom of the ages from one generation to the next.

One of my current enterprises (a few years in the working now, really) is to develop a repertory of demonstrations and visual aids to present and then to ask, figuratively if not literally, "What did you see?" Or "What do you think you saw? Why did that happen?" Or simply "What happened? Let's think this through together. What do you still need to know? Let me supply this additional bit of information; now what can you say?"

(3) Love your discipline. My current course is called Natural Science. ("Natural" from the Latin verb meaning "to be born"—i.e., in the primitive mind, "all that is." "Science" from the Latin verb meaning "to know.") So it is knowing all that is. What a wonderful opportunity. What a fabulous adventure. What a magnificent task. One of my patrons in this enterprise is the twelfth-century monk Hugh of St. Victor, who is quoted as saying, "Learn everything. Nothing is wasted."

Since all knowledge is connected, science is connected to culture, humanities, history, languages, literature, philosophy, theology, everything. And so all other disciplines are similarly interconnected. Maybe my exhortation to "Love your discipline" really should be to "Love knowledge."

So much to know. So much yet to learn. So much to teach. And so little time to learn it all. Thank God for the hope of eternity, eh?

Father Leopold Keffler

Great Teachers and Dead Sharks

Michael Flachmann

Most of us know superb teaching when we see it. The problem, of course, is being able to duplicate these skills in our own classrooms. Simply watching Lindsay Davenport hit a topspin backhand down the line or LeBron James nail a twenty footer from the top of the key doesn't guarantee we'll be able to perform the same athletic feats ourselves. Like the mastery of any mystery, becoming a great teacher takes patience, practice, and a lot of innate creativity.

Having taught at the college level for over thirty years, I've had the opportunity to observe many first-rate professors in a wide variety of academic disciplines. I've also made more than my fair share of pedagogical mistakes. As a result, I think I've gained some important insights into the talent necessary for excellence in the college classroom—especially in the areas of professional commitment, research and publication, work habits, relationships with students, and job satisfaction. Based on this experience, therefore, I'd like to offer here a few modest proposals for becoming a great teacher.

Professional Commitment

First of all, the very best teachers are hopelessly, profoundly, inextricably invested in their areas of expertise. They drone on at cocktail parties about the inherent evils of deforestation; they scribble obtuse mathematical formulas on napkins at their daughters' soccer games; and they haunt out-of-the-way bookstores in hopes of discovering a long-lost tome on some obscure seventeenth-century German physicist. They go to sleep dreaming about Piaget and wake up thinking about him. They are, in fact, always just a heartbeat away from the subject they love, because it lives not only in their heads but in the blood coursing through their veins. In short, they are deeply and passionately involved in what they teach. Although the love of one's subject isn't always sufficient to guarantee that a teacher will be great, it's the right place to start.

This passion for our chosen academic area must be coupled with the innate ability to communicate that material clearly and enthusiastically to our students in a fashion that helps them understand, viscerally as well as intellectually, why we care so deeply about Shakespeare or differential equations or Irish political history or whatever topics we're spending our professional lives with. Ironically, I think the intensity of graduate training and the rigors inherent in the repetitive nature of our profession conspire over time to strip away much of the excitement that brought us to our chosen fields in the first place. I remember that I had to work for a few years after earning my Ph.D. before I could shed the seriousness of doctoral studies and replace it with the cheerful pragmatism of teaching at the college level. Consequently, I have done my best to rediscover that original passion and to share it unashamedly with my students, to convince them not only with my head but with my heart as well that they too can experience the unique joy of my cherished academic field.

Excellent teachers also need to find their proper instructional level. I know people, as I'm sure we all do, who are brilliant college professors but would do an absolutely horrid job in front of junior high school kids. Conversely, I've met some fine kindergarten teachers who would be hopelessly out of place in a college classroom. Though some folks might argue that great teachers can convey any subject in any academic environment, I disagree. We've all got to find the right educational milieu to accommodate our individual talents, interests, and goals in life. Although I think I'm a good college professor, I would have failed miserably at the high school level. I'm just not patient enough to deal with the emotional and intellectual traumas of tenth graders five days a week. In fact, whenever I do a guest stint in a high school classroom, I'm always exhausted afterwards. I greatly admire teachers who perform this feat for their entire professional lives! College is where my heart lies, however, and I'm glad I discovered this personal truth early in my teaching career.

Research and Publication

In addition, great teachers need to stay alive intellectually. Remember Woody Allen's memorable lines to Diane Keaton in *Annie Hall:* "A relationship . . . is like a shark. . . . It has to constantly move forward or it dies. And I think what we've got on our hands is a dead shark." In order to "move forward" in our profession, we have to stay current with our academic reading, attend conferences, and, yes, churn out those books and articles. We can't expect our students to be good writers at their level if we aren't good writers at ours. Publications are pragmatic proof that we have not turned into dead sharks, that we care enough about our research to share it with colleagues at home and abroad, and that we aren't relying on yellowed, dog-eared, twenty-year-old lecture notes when we ought to be expounding exciting new theories to a fresh generation of students.

I've been fortunate to pursue research that has supported my teaching and publications at the same time. I'm particularly happy, I admit, when a symbiotic relationship exists between my work in the classroom and my time in the study. Especially fulfilling are the occasions when I can involve students in my own professional work, as I do at the Utah Shakespearean Festival, where I have been company dramaturg for the past twenty summers. I can't think of a greater thrill, in fact, than seeing one of my students watch a first-rate Shakespeare production for which she has provided crucial theatrical research on Richard III's historical coronation ceremony, the ducal crest for the Doge of Venice, or the sylvan geography of the Forest of Arden. This practical use of theoretical knowledge helps bridge the gap between the classroom and the "real world" and provides our students with the skill and confidence to succeed during the rest of their lives.

Work Habits

Another crucial ingredient in this successful educational stew is making certain our own pedagogical flaws don't inhibit the progress of our students. Needless to say, we must be well organized, punctual, patient, courteous, free from bias, energetic, and completely dedicated to student success. By the same token, we should avoid arrogance, vanity, egotism, cockiness, and intimidation. We also need to prepare conscientiously for class, return graded papers in a timely fashion, hold regular office hours, answer student phone calls and e-mails promptly, and resist the sometimes overwhelming temptation to belittle anyone in class. Furthermore, most great teachers infuse a lively, tasteful sense of humor into the classroom experience in order to keep interest levels high and foster an open and encouraging environment where student comments are warmly solicited and genuinely rewarded. Good teachers who lack a substantial number of the qualities listed above do their students a serious disservice in the learning process.

I've also learned several important lessons over the years by watching the very best teachers at our university pull more than their fair share of the department workload. We're all familiar with the faculty prima donnas who dash in to teach their classes, then disappear into the library to continue research on their next seminal book or article. These professorial "ghosts" may think they're much more important than the rest of us, but all they really do is build up resentment among other faculty members who have to take up the slack in advising students, serving on committees, writing reports, and tending to all the other business crucial to a well-run department. The top teachers I know, therefore, will never be found hiding behind closed office doors. Great professors are those who teach brilliantly, publish frequently, and still have time to perform their departmental duties with a cheerful, positive attitude. To do anything less is disrespectful to the students we serve and the colleagues with whom we work.

Relationships with Students

In addition, top teachers are always uniquely aware of their students' needs, both inside and outside the classroom. I've never met a truly great professor

47

who didn't sincerely enjoy the students he or she was teaching. Although such pleasure depends in large part on the grade levels we are most comfortable with, it is also influenced by a host of other variables that intersect with each professor's own personal background. Affection for the students we teach begets sensitivity to their distinct and idiosyncratic learning styles, which must be taken into account if we are to be successful at initiating them into the secrets of our academic disciplines. I confess that I am always happiest when I am surrounded by students, either walking together with them on campus or sitting around my office with them discussing the devotional poetry of John Donne, the bloody denouement of *Titus Andronicus,* or the wide variety of courses in next fall's class schedule. If we truly care about our students—as people and as individuals—we simply won't let them fail. And that's a certain formula for success.

Caring about our students in the classroom also means we are more likely to allow them "ownership" of knowledge. As a result, the best teachers I know seldom lecture. They may orchestrate, lead, cajole, prod, or persuade, but they never preach, proclaim, sermonize, or dominate. In theatrical terms, it's the difference between a monologue and a dialogue. Great teachers involve their students in the ownership of truth by getting them up and out of their seats so they can experience and internalize knowledge rather than having it force-fed to them through reading books and listening passively to lectures. Instead of showing our students how smart *we* are through witty diatribes in class, we need to let them understand how smart *they* are through the use of interactive learning techniques that involve everyone physically, emotionally, and intellectually in the educational process. I believe that the locus of knowledge resides in the students and that the professor's job is to help them discover the answers to life's problems within themselves. Only then can they truly possess the knowledge we are paid to teach them. I have to admit this was one of the most difficult concepts I learned in order to become a better teacher. Most people want others to see them as intelligent, and the teaching profession offers a convenient opportunity for us all to preen before our adoring pupils. I finally had to accept the fact, however, that parading my own wit and charm in the classroom was counterproductive to the educational process. As a result, I always try to conduct classes that are centered on the students, because their intellectual development is the primary reason all of us are there.

Similarly, great teachers also extend their relationships with students beyond the classroom. I've tried to follow that advice on my own campus, where I not only teach in the English department, but I also chair the university honors program, instruct classes in Judo and self-defense, and serve as an assistant coach for our women's intercollegiate tennis team. In my opinion, an immense amount of learning takes place outside the university walls, especially during study groups, excursions to course-related activities, parties, and faculty office hours; consequently, I have always cherished the extracurricular contact I have with students. The relatively few minutes I spend with them in class, which reveal only a CAT-scan slice of their lives, don't provide nearly enough time for me to know them as individuals. Nor will this limited in-class exposure encourage any but the most desperately troubled students to seek me out for assistance with their problems. I can count on one hand the number of people who have done poorly in my classes because they weren't intelligent enough to survive. The vast majority of students who make low grades, I've discovered, do so principally because of financial, social, or physical problems that must be solved before the students can be successful. Through our roles as advisors and counselors, we can help people become good students; solve difficult and sometimes life-threatening dilemmas; choose rewarding careers; and lead happier, more fulfilling lives. All it takes is a little time and effort outside the classroom.

Job Satisfaction

Finally, the very best teachers genuinely enjoy their jobs. Someone once said that you're happy in your career if you're never quite certain whether you're working or playing. Not surprisingly, excellent teachers always appear to be enjoying themselves tremendously. Sure, they get irritated by students at times; sure, paper grading can be oppressive; sure, salaries need to be raised; and sure, faculty meetings are often a bore. But the great professors invariably spend much less time *kvetching* than the rest of us mere mortals. They seem to instinctively realize, in a way other teachers do not, that they have been afforded the rare privilege of spending their lives helping students learn the hidden truths of life. What greater honor and responsibility could we have than "leading others out of themselves"—which is, after all, what the word *education* means. The best teachers, therefore, make learning an enormous amount of fun for their students. As a result, they always seem to be having a lot of fun too.

Conclusion

So these are my suggestions for becoming a great teacher. If you agree, I'm delighted. If not, I'd encourage you to create your own agenda and follow it conscientiously. Teaching is too complex and challenging an occupation to tackle without a master plan of some kind. We owe it to our students and to ourselves to consider seriously how we perform this sacred mystery. The sea of education has far too many dead sharks without adding one more to the population!

Michael Flachmann

Teaching Writing: A Collage

Libby Falk Jones

> It is not terror that fosters learning, it is hope.
>
> —Mike Rose, *Lives on the Boundary*

I. Evolution of a (Writing) Teacher: Three Critical Moments

One: I learn to learn.

Fall 1967: My first semester of grad school in English at SUNY Stony Brook. My hardest class (though none of them is easy): Eighteenth-Century Literature—Boswell and Johnson, with Professor Thomas Rogers. He seems nice, like Jiminy Cricket—calls us respectfully by our last names, using "Miss" and "Mrs." accurately—but I'm terrified. Sure, I had a good undergraduate record at a good school—but as a history major. Plus I've been out of school for a year, writing copy for a pharmaceutical company and reading novels on my lunch breaks. My motivation is strong—I know I love literature and I'm eager to learn—but my ignorance is deep. Stuart, from Brandeis, has read everything, twice. Saul, from SUNY Albany, is already teaching. A transplanted southerner, I don't think I fit.

If I stick it out in grad school, one day I'll be up there at the blackboard, so I watch all my professors with a new consciousness. The second day of class is on Johnson's *Rambler* 151. Mr. Rogers calls on me to state the thesis. I have "read" the assignment—passing my eyes over the pages—but have not grasped its heart. Even more shameful, I'm not familiar with the term "thesis." Mr. Rogers explains that it's the conclusion, what Johnson wants us to take away from the essay. Should I just say I don't know? Some native gumption won't let me give up so easily. "May I have a minute to look at the essay?" "Sure." I skim the piece, noting points, then focus in on the concluding paragraph. A main idea leaps out: "Man should examine his life." A thesis is a conclusion, right? Hesitantly, I state Johnson's idea. Without changing expression or commenting, Mr. Rogers writes it on the board. I'm embarrassed—it looks so bold, there. Is it right? Mr. Rogers asks me for my evidence. He asks others what they think. Some suggest substitutions. He writes those on the board, too. I consider each suggestion, looking back carefully at the essay. Those points are there, but none is the controlling idea. I point this out. When the speaker accepts my reasoning,

Mr. Rogers erases that point from the board. At the end of the period, my thesis still stands. Now I see how that thesis controls the essay, how Johnson's subpoints lay its groundwork. My classmates and I have inquired together into the argument and structure of the essay, confirming and deepening my original insight. I have learned to stick my neck out, to support what I say, to consider others' viewpoints. How has Mr. Rogers taught us? He has asked questions. He has not given us answers. We have figured them out for ourselves, in dialogue.

Next week comes our first essay: describe the character of the Rambler. This won't be a single sentence, right or wrong. I read lots of *Rambler* essays. The Rambler comes alive for me, a moral fellow, caring at his core, wise and sometimes harsh, a little tendentious and pretentious. I draw some conclusions and support them with citations, worrying all along that my efforts will be inadequate. When Mr. Rogers returns our papers, we eagerly flip through the pages. I see comments in the margins of my classmates' work; mine has only a half-page of comments at the end, in Mr. Rogers's fine, controlled hand. "This is admirably done," he begins, going on to name all the things I have done well: reading beyond our texts to find telling evidence to support my points, developing and qualifying my meaning so carefully that he has not had to pursue my thinking in the margins of my piece, quoting accurately and to the point. It has not occurred to me that a writer would not do these things. Mr. Rogers's naming and affirming these scholarly habits lifts them to the level of strategies I will use again and again and later teach to others. Even more important: reading his comments, I know that despite my lack of appropriate preparation, I can succeed in graduate school. That essential affirmation carries me through challenging courses, difficult written and oral examinations, and the seven-year writing of a dissertation.

Two: I learn to teach.

Spring 1968: Most of the other graduate students are teaching their own classes. I watch them with envy. They devise and share clever writing assignments on essays in the *Norton Reader,* a new assignment every two weeks. They spend lots of time marking papers. They have power, authority. Chatting after a seminar, one TA brandishes a red rubber stamp, "BULLSHIT!" with which she peppers her students' papers. Others laugh, agreeing that this is a good means of deflating these arrogant New Yorkers. I know instinctively that I could not teach that way.

The university begins a new program, where graduate students serve as tutors in residence halls. I have done OK fall term, so I'm hired to sit two evenings a week in the ground-floor parlor of a women's dormitory, available to help any of the residents. Finally a young woman stops in. An earnest Long Islander in her first year, she has to write a paper on an Emily Dickinson poem.

She doesn't understand the poem. And it's only thirteen lines—how will she get five hundred words on it?

I have no easy answer. I've never read the poem myself, don't know much about Dickinson. As an authority, I'm a failure. What can we do? Together we look at the poem. She reads it aloud. We talk through Dickinson's ideas, noticing each word and thinking about how that particular word contributes to the poem's meaning. We try substituting antonyms, then synonyms. We begin to see subtleties in Dickinson's language. With our voices, we exaggerate the punctuation, seeing subtleties there too. An hour passes quickly. Years later, I'll recite that poem—"After great pain, a formal feeling comes . . ."—as I labor with my first child.

Next week she's back and brings a friend. Soon my eight hours are all filled. I talk with students about the texts they are exploring. I help them understand their assignments and their teachers' comments on their writing. I'm an evaluator rather than a grader, a coach whose authority comes from my understanding of their bewilderment in the face of unfamiliar things, from the questions I ask rather than the answers I give, from the ways I can help them as readers and writers articulate what they already know and the ways I can encourage them to entertain new ideas.

My more than thirty years of teaching—in and out of the classroom—will be informed by this early conferencing experience, where I walk with learners one by one along their paths.

Three: I become a writing teacher.

Fall 1977: Four schools and one child later, still at work on my dissertation—a rhetorical study of two nineteenth-century fictions—I find myself teaching freshman composition as an adjunct instructor at the University of Tennessee, Knoxville. I am part of the freshman English program shaped by the legendary John Hodges, author of the *Harbrace College Handbook,* a standard in the composition field. Texts—imaginative, expository, and argumentative—are and continue to be central to my teaching. At Tennessee, my focus shifts. Before, I was a teacher of literature who used and also taught writing. Now I become a writing teacher who (often) uses literature.

This shift results largely from my own interests. I love the growth I see in my composition students—growth in insights, creativity, ability to express themselves, ability to think and argue. I love the fact that writing involves the whole person—head, heart, and spirit. As a teacher, I love the freedom teaching writing gives me: I can stay true to my subject while inventing new approaches, topics, texts, and assignments. In fact, my subject demands this flexibility, calls forth responsive teaching. A writing teacher quickly discovers that active learning

53

is the only kind there is: writers have to write. Collaborative learning is also a given: writers have to have responses from their audiences. I thrive on the improvisational teaching that follows from these basic truths.

And after a decade of teaching writing—of experiencing the challenges as well as the joys—I see the need to theorize my practice, to discover better ways of teaching what's always been English teachers' daily bread. Tennessee takes writing seriously, the freshman staff has meetings, people talk about genres and pedagogies of writing, they share theories as well as assignments. I soon see that this local conversation is part of a larger one: composition and its philosophical framework, rhetoric, is emerging as a scholarly field. I read, I talk. I read Britton and Kinneavy and Bruffee and Elbow and Berthoff and Flower. I come to understand and appreciate the three primary composition theories—expressivist, cognitivist, and social-constructionist—each the others' opposite but, paradoxically, all true. My practices flow from these theories as well as from my growing experience as a teacher of composition—a valid knowledge source, what Stephen North (in *The Making of Knowledge in Composition*) calls "practitioner lore."

My teaching of writing helps me find new strategies for analyzing the texts in my dissertation; I finish it with strong reader evaluations. I publish my own students' writings in a class booklet and offer to edit a collection of good writing in the freshman English program, to become a text for students the next year. I help to plan a revised first-year writing curriculum and in it teach new writing courses, one on language and argument, one on technical writing. I begin my first research project on writing, a study of assignment design and invention strategies in Tennessee's first-term course. I begin attending and presenting at national conferences. I propose an experimental writing class, one based entirely on conferencing. I edit the handbook for instructors in the freshman English program. I design a study of teachers' approaches to nonsexist language in composition classes. I help develop and teach a sophomore course in creative writing. I develop an approach to teaching critical thinking and argumentative writing, and I study its effects.

And after ten years (and another child), I'm ready to move to a full-time position centered on writing and the teaching of writing.

In teaching writing, I use everything I've ever learned. And I keep learning, every term, every day. For me, teaching writing holds what Parker Palmer terms the two essentials of good teaching: love of learning and love of learners. Being a writing teacher holds me to a high standard of knowledge and practice. As a writing teacher, what I do matters. I have found a vocation.

54

II. Teaching Writing: True Poems

Cat Cinquain

The cat
sits on a pile
of papers. Muffled by
fur, words creep out. *Sacramental.*
Crayon.

Class Dream

I am teaching
a class in
writing. My
son is there,
age four. Some
new students—
a gray-haired
woman with glasses
and a one-year-old
in diapers. As I
give the lesson,
the baby totters
to the desk
to suck my fingers.

I shake my
son's shoulders until,
flushed red, I
look down to
see my body
bleed bright
green.

The Writing Teacher's Invocation

> I'm a bag lady
> A bag of tricks lady
> Give a word
>   Find a place
>   See that line
> May my energy sizzle
> Your opaque eyes

Song for the Class

> You give me your poems,
> your souls on the pages.
> You want to make meanings:
> I only hear sounds.
>
> Your souls on the pages:
> arias, drumbeats.
> I only hear sounds:
> I don't know your meanings.
>
> Arias, drumbeats
> at the hearts of your poems.
> I don't know your meanings.
> I do know your souls.
>
> At the hearts of your poems
> are your meanings in sounds.
> I do know your souls when
> you give me your poems.

The Co-Creative Classroom

April Morgan

I sat in the passenger seat of classrooms for years, assessing and absorbing my teachers' ways. I was raring to go when, unexpectedly, I was offered a chance to teach international law in graduate school.

One day, I wore a new skirt, white shirt, and an unbuttoned, black blazer; there was a healthy gap between the jacket flaps. I had scraped my hair back and up to make me look older so that the students wouldn't know I was only a couple of years their senior. Experienced professor that I was trying to make them believe I was, I walked around the small room, making eye contact with each of my sixteen students to be sure they were with me as I explained the intricacies of treaty reservations I had memorized in detail the night before.

As I looked into the eyes of a student whom I had been trying to coax out of his silence, I felt a loosening of my right bra strap. I kept talking. It shifted again, dangerously. Then, as I stood two feet away from the Italian bird-watcher who was only beginning to feel comfortable speaking in class, I broke into the kind of laughter Mary Tyler Moore let loose at Peanut the Clown's funeral. Although I was horrified with myself, I could not stop. The class watched, having no idea what the problem was and too polite to ask. I had to call a time-out by waving and sweeping my hands out the door to indicate a break.

Class resumed, still without a word of explanation from me; I was afraid that if I explained (and how would I do that?) I'd start laughing again. To my amazement, my students never seemed to hold it against me. I don't remember what my evaluations said, but they couldn't have been that bad, because I was asked to teach again. I understood then that my approach to the class had been unnecessarily laced with fear of my students, anxiety rooted in the certainty of my ignorance. I found that I could afford to lighten up a little, to develop my own style. This incident was also one of my early indicators that students tend to be quite forgiving of teachers' flubs in an otherwise well-run class. My students' generosity continues to impress me.

One of the most helpful tips I ever received was delivered a few years later, when an observer showed up to evaluate a class I was not well prepared for. When he introduced himself before class, I admitted my lack of preparation to lower his expectations (and mine). He cheerily responded, "Oh, well, those are usually the best classes!" It dawned on me that he wasn't just being gracious. He was serious. I realized that I had inadvertently raised his expectations. Since it was hopeless, I decided that we would at least have fun with the material—no matter how little of it I could remember. My observer was right. We got into a groove; the conversation seemed effortless and productive.

Something I thought I already knew crystallized more clearly in my mind at that point. I realized that too often lecture notes that help us articulate in our own minds exactly what we want to communicate become stories we have told so many times we no longer experience their content ourselves; we're on autopilot and we don't even know it at first. This kind of passive teaching drains a class of energy.

On the other hand, co-creating a lesson makes a class pop and sparkle as in the movie *Dead Poets Society.* One of my favorite scenes occurs when Professor John Keating, the teacher played by Robin Williams, directs his astonished students to rip out the pages of a boring literary analysis from their English books. To encourage them to believe that meaningful words belong to them as much as to the so-called experts and that being insightful doesn't require using a highbrow vocabulary, Keating guides the class's destruction of their safety net. After the teacher's putting himself on the line this way and making room for his students' self-expression, his shyest student later extemporaneously composes a poem about the "sweaty-toothed madman," Walt Whitman.

Teaching is about the students. Increasingly, I put potentially useful concepts and activities in front of students for them to work and play with, to get myself and their ideas about passive learning out of the way.

Rearranging the learning architecture of my classroom this way does not entail relaxing clear, firm boundaries. Beyond the basics—like not touching students or socializing with them—I take precautions when grading. No one wants to be identified as a number, unless being identified by name leads to an unfair result. Decision-making research indicates that people tend to hold assumptions about others on the basis of the most fleeting, flimsy impressions. Further, it suggests that we maintain these assumptions in spite of new information to the contrary. Somehow, we manage to conscientiously assimilate incoming data in a way that reinforces our original perceptions. Teachers are not immune, so I ask students not to put their names on exams and papers. Instead, they use their social security numbers, which I later match to names as

I record the grades. If you think you do not have such assumptions about your students—or that you can effectively control them—try this: have students take exams by social security numbers only—no names—and guess whose exam you think you are grading as you work through the pile, writing down names in pencil somewhere as you go. Then, compare your expectations with actual performances. If you are surprised even once, you have something to guard against in grading in order to be as fair as possible. A graduate student of mine recently took this challenge and came back saying, "You're right. . . . When I liked someone, I found myself making excuses for them, thinking, 'I know she really meant to say. . . .'"

Years ago, I stood next to figure-skating guru Robert Unger as we watched one of his most accomplished students, Jon Robinson, skate in a regional competition. The home audience was excited and nervous because Jon was so good that he hadn't had competition in years. As we watched the skaters warm up, we realized that the competitor was going to give Jon a run for his money. The out-of-towner demonstrated impressive technical skills; each trick he performed was a textbook illustration of what the spin or jump should look like. Jon, too, presented a program of nearly flawless maneuvers. I turned worried eyes to Mr. Unger, thinking it was unclear who had won, but he just smiled, confident that it was obvious. He was right; the distinction went to the person who did all his moves with heart, who knew that mastery of technical skills is just the beginning and it's what they are put in service of that matters. This is what turns science into art. Similarly, despite the value academia places on the intellect, it is not an end in itself in my eyes.

What else is teaching if not support for the students' highest development? It is in this sense and only in this professional, appropriate, hands-off manner that I love my students; I want the best for them and out of them, given their goals for themselves.

So after discussing what we think we know, I ask students what the material means for them, how and why they might do things differently, what wisdom comes to them from what they have studied. As soon as they can use the word *I*, even the most abstract material becomes personal for them. This identification goes a long way toward establishing relevance in the subject matter for the student. This exercise is meant to prompt students to ask what I consider to be the most important questions in relation to everything we study: "Who am I in relation to this? Is this an expression of my values? If not, what would be?"

Students want reassurance that I literally intend for them to use the first person. They give me the impression that *I* has been all but made illegal in many

61

institutions of learning. This suggests to me that many of us prioritize the dead and dying over life and the living, what was over what could be. Students deserve opportunities to practice shaping the world according to their wishes and to be challenged on questionable prescriptions they present as much as they deserve to know why things are the way they are. Active learning—in which students shoulder a significant degree of the responsibility for the construction of knowledge—creates spaces in which this can occur. In 1907, another Ph.D. interested in international politics put it this way:

> There is a great deal of information to be communicated to the pupil, a great deal of mere drill in which he is to be exercised and disciplined. . . . But education is not, after all, when properly viewed, an affair of filling and furnishing the mind, but a business of informing the spirit; and nothing affects spirit but spirit. . . . The personal factor in education is the chief factor. . . . No system of teaching which depends upon methods and not upon persons, or which imagines the possibility of any substitution of the written word for the living person, can work any but mechanical effects.[1]

At its most basic, what we call active learning simply invites students to bring more of themselves to the educational process than the reproduction of text and lecture content requires. In my experience, active learning facilitates directing attention to motivations, meanings, and implications that can otherwise be easily over-looked or grasped only at a surface level of awareness. Role-playing simulations and first-person narratives seem to afford special opportunities to move beyond explaining world affairs to promote understanding of them.

Nonetheless, despite the benefits of this approach, students who appear to enjoy this kind of learning environment have a limited tolerance for how much class time and individual effort they are willing to devote to such activities. Further, some students—often those with stellar academic records and clear career goals—adamantly resist this format altogether. Given this range of learning styles and educational objectives, I usually incorporate just one major active learning module into a syllabus. However, each day I strive to engage learning through discussion.

Now, when speaking with graduate students about the work in front of them, I share a few practical tips and some recent research. If performance anxiety grips someone, I talk about my awkward moments. I emphasize what I learned

The Co-Creative Classroom

from them and how I altered what I do as a result. In a seminar, I also ask rising scholars what their goals are for themselves and for their students in relation to specific material and listen to how they intend to get there. If someone in the group identifies a potential problem, we pitch in to explore options and evaluate possible outcomes, almost as though planning an old-fashioned barn-raising. Throughout, we suggest resources and take care to identify what we believe in as well as what stirs doubt.

Note

1. Excerpts from Woodrow Wilson, "The Personal Factor in Education," *The Youth's Companion* 81 (Sep. 12, 1907): 423–24. Reprinted in Arthur S. Link, ed., *The Papers of Woodrow Wilson* (Princeton, N.J.: Princeton University Press, 1974), vol. 17: 326, 332, 333.

Reflections from the World of Ice-Skating

Robert Unger

Over the more than fifty years that I have been teaching ice-skating, I have learned more from my students than they have learned from me. Maybe the most important thing my students have taught me is this: people are either in "sending mode" or in "receiving mode," and in my experience, most listeners are in "sending mode" during a teacher's presentation. That is, they are already preparing their answers or what they are going to "send" back to you instead of listening. Because they aren't truly receiving, they are making what you are actually saying fit what they expect you to say. In order to be sure that they have truly received, you have to repeat yourself quite a lot. I have found that in most cases, if I don't say it five times, it doesn't sink in. So I either find a way to say something five times or I don't say it at all. Even then, it isn't a sure thing, but repetition greatly increases my chances of being heard. Another reason to say something many times is that students often will not tell me when they do not understand, because they think admitting this makes them look like fools. If I keep coming back to something they don't understand, they are more likely to admit their confusion.

I am aware that the same terminology does not work with all students. I have condensed my terminology over the years and learned to stick to those words that work best, keeping in mind that each person needs a different terminology to understand the same point. I may say the same thing five times in one lesson to one person, but I also have to be able to express that same concept in many other ways so that other people can understand it.

As a coach, one of my mantras is that "practice does *not* make perfect; *correct* practice makes perfect." Actually, there is no such thing as perfect; learners improve and move closer to perfection without ever attaining it. How does one practice in order to make progress toward perfection? In ice-skating, we use correct practice to create a "body memory." When I am teaching a student, I have him walk through the motions of a move in front of me so that I can see that he or she is practicing it correctly and developing the correct body memory. I stress that this walking exercise—or "walker"—has to be done in the required pacing of the move.

Hopefully, when the student later practices alone, he or she will do the exercise the same way he or she did it in the lesson. Having students practice correctly in front of you to develop the correct body memory is very important because otherwise they may diligently practice incorrectly by themselves and then develop the wrong body memory. Once this incorrect habit is formed, it is hard to break. So if something is not working in practice, I encourage students to do something else! Stop working on what is not going well. Do something that feels good, and then come back to the other thing later. In my own training, I waited to be sure I could feel what I was doing in my stomach. If I couldn't feel it there, it wasn't right, and I went on to something else and came back to what I was working on later when the feeling was there. Then it worked!

In the methodology of correct practice, students should be able to evaluate what they do. They should be able to diagnose their performances themselves. They should be able to accurately explain why something went wrong as well as why something went right. I tell skaters to practice together because one person can apply the theory that I taught the group as a whole to the person who is doing the maneuver. They take turns observing one another, being sure the body memory being developed is correct even when they are practicing away from me. They learn to evaluate themselves this way, too. Students also learn by watching, evaluating, and teaching others more than they learn from merely listening to me.

Another one of my sayings is that "less is more." In order to create a body memory, teachers have to learn not to overteach. Don't detail your point to death.

One day I videoed my best, top-level jumpers. Using a timer, I found they were in the air for three-quarters of one second. How much can anybody think about in such a short time? Instead of the mind, Mother Nature must take over. This means not thinking or using the mind to achieve the proper form but letting the correct body memory take over and do it for you. Don't handicap a student's mind by asking him to think about correct technique that should have been learned in the walk-through exercises. When someone tries too hard, it shows. It burdens the mind. Perhaps a skater can think of one thing in each move. I learned the double loop when I let go; I learned it and I didn't even know what had happened. It was just there one day. If the mind is free, a skater can think about presentation, which is an appropriate thing to focus on.

For example, every jump flows through five stages: (1) approach, (2) take-off, (3) rotation, (4) preparation for landing, and (5) landing/gliding out of the move. To teach all five stages of the jump at once overburdens the mind. Making students think too much actually works against creating a body memory because such overload activates and gives priority to the brain instead of to bodily instincts. Teach the middle three steps until the student can do the jump; then, once the body memory or habit is solidly and correctly formed, you can explain the other two steps in more detail. This focus on the body reflects the fact that students learn by doing, not by my talking, no matter how much I know or how well I palaver.

Over the years, I have learned that students with limited capability who work hard go farther than those who have lots of talent but no idea what to do with it. I have many memories of lovely, natural skaters who could learn a new move very easily and who could spontaneously make up a beautiful routine to any music I put on. These talented skaters were usually the same ones who came late to class, never warmed up, didn't practice in between lessons, and couldn't remember the beautiful routines they had just made up if I asked to see them a second time. It was the skaters who lacked this natural talent but practiced as I taught them to who developed into the best skaters and went the farthest. Despite being very aware of this, I am still pleasantly surprised when I see people I think will never be any good turn from ugly ducklings into beautiful swans. Another benefit of being a hard worker is that those who are learn to overcome any obstacle in their way, whereas mere talent drops out of the picture when obstacles occur. However, talent *and* hard work are needed to get to the high, high levels. Hard work alone is not enough.

As for people with natural talent, for those who get it right the first time without having to hear your instruction, leave them alone. Don't go in and explain to them what they are already doing right. This only makes them self-conscious. Mother Nature is already at work. Let her do her work. Once the body memory is set, then you can discuss the details. Jump in with this too early, and these natural talents are sometimes never able to get it right again.

A good mind-set for all kinds of learners should include being in a good mood and a receptive mood. Work *with* the teacher. Don't be thinking about how you're going to respond; just be with the teacher. This is especially true for beginners. If they trust you and do what feels at first counterintuitive to them, they'll get past this point to discover their natural balance.

Golf's Learning Mind

Michael Hebron

During the first half of my career as a golf instructor, I tried to learn all I could about the golf swing and playing the game. My business as a golf instructor was growing, and I began to train other instructors for the PGA of America and several PGA organizations in Europe, Canada, and Japan. I was very fortunate to have my work recognized by the Professional Golfers' Association of America, receiving two of its national awards. *Golf Magazine* named me one of America's top fifty teachers.

Then one day I had one of those "Ah!" moments that are a gift from somewhere. I realized that some bright and able people who were taking lessons from me were always asking for the same advice. I realized then that they were not experiencing any long-term learning because I did not know how to help people retain insights that were personal in nature. So over the next fifteen years, I tried to become more familiar with the nature of learning. I immersed myself in research on the science of learning. What I discovered is that there is an ideal learning environment I call the "flow state." Here are some of its primary principles, which are applicable to any field.

Golf's first instruction book, *The Golfer's Manual,* was published in 1857; today, expert opinion is readily available from books, videos, TV shows and private lessons. Golf equipment (clubs and balls) and the field of play (grass and playing conditions) have improved over the past 150 years. You would think that with all these improvements the average United States Golf Association handicap should have gone down over time, but statistics show it has not. What causes this lack of progress? My guess is that it is because what most people believe about teaching and learning actually fragments or disables long-term learning.

There is a tendency in our culture to create heroes—especially in sports. Many people use their heroes as models; they attempt to copy their styles and look to them for guidance. But this very human tendency can slow down progress when it comes to learning golf. Golfers should always see themselves and be seen as individuals. This is because while there are a few (not many) important essentials, every champion applies these essentials in his or her own best way. Clever, often conflicting advice in an era of information overload can distract golfers from developing workable insights about core golf knowledge and self-discovery. This makes progress more difficult than it has to be.

Dale Carnegie, author of *How to Win Friends and Influence People*, said, "The only way to win an argument is to avoid it." Ironically (considering the source of this good advice), "how-to" instructions are, for golfers, much like arguments: best avoided. Each set of "how-to" instructions contradicts the last. Golfers who want to experience long-term progress should avoid the disagreements and arguments these contradictory instructions offer. Any breakthrough a golfer is capable of making requires a breakaway from noisy arguments about who is right and who is wrong. Our goal is a nonverbal reality that only a silent mind can achieve. Until the mind is free of others' "how-to" advice, it is almost impossible to gain the personal insights necessary to solve problems.

Playing golf is about solving problems. For a golfer to shoot 90, he or she will have to face ninety different problems to solve. Some problems are short, some are long, some are up, some are down, some are out of sand, some are from the grass, some from the woods, and some from short grass. But in total there are ninety problems to solve. People who are playing good golf have the confidence and trust in their self- awareness of the basic physics of golf to adapt their styles of play to the shot at hand in a more workable manner than poor golfers do. They are *proactive* with their environments rather than *reactive* to directions.

All of the problems mentioned above are addressed by the First Principle of Golf. It holds that the foundation of golf is the appropriate alignment and application of force through impact for a given environment. This foundational principle is responsible for all outcomes, and it must be taken into consideration by golfers who want to develop the ability to predict the outcome of their swings and ball flights. So every shot begins with this basic question: "How do I want the club shaft, clubface, and club head to be aligned through impact for the shot at hand?"

People often believe that their lack of progress is because of their own shortcomings or lack of physical skills; unfortunately they overlook how they have been trying to learn by taking direction from or imitating others. People who are not making progress should keep the following in mind: the foundation of long-term progress is personal experience. This fundamental truth about interacting with environments is overlooked by both givers and receivers of advice when how-to instructions, drills, and expert models are used for learning. How-to instructions can sometimes provide a quick fix, but long-term progress is not concerned with immediate results. How-to instructions manage golfers. Self-learning and awareness skills educate golfers so that they can begin with a result in mind—based on the shot at hand—and determine and apply the most effective application of force.

I see myself as a learning coach who helps people attain "golf smarts" by pointing out factors about the environment they may not have noticed. "Are you aware that this green is angled slightly uphill?" I ask. Together, we map the environment because doing so yields results we can learn from. Balls do not *try* to roll fast to hills, they just do. Nine irons do not try to go higher than five irons, they just do. Then we come up with a workable blueprint for the shot at hand based on our map and nature's laws that guide all golfers. As we interact with the environment and notice the outcome, we learn without effort. If the result is not everything we'd like, we adjust the plan based on personal experience and insight. In such settings, when there is a silence in the mind, without "how-to" judgments, we can become fully aware of the shot at hand and determine what is and is not required in order to achieve the desired result.

Unfortunately, what the golf instruction community has to offer is mostly a large volume of unconnected how-to instructions that are void of core golf knowledge or prerequisite information. The information base I use today has been gathered over the last thirty-five years with the help and support of people from the research and application sides of many disciplines, including engineering, education, biomechanics, and the arts to name a few. Without workable insights into learning golf smarts, golfers are often passive learners following someone else's advice, which gives them a false sense of confidence that falls apart on the course. Whenever there is an attempt to "give" a lesson, progress will be slower than when lessons are "gained" through personal experiences.

We can all become learning-disabled when task requirements exceed our proficiency. We reach a stress point when information, quick decisions, or competing distractions will derail our attention.

Strengths and weaknesses, habits of attention, emotional blocks, frustration, and recovery behaviors are exposed at this stress point. Meaning drops off, vision contracts, and hearing dims in different ways for each person. Some who lose their sequence, direction, or rhythm can recover and succeed; others become confused and can't. People forget, forfeit, and fall defeated in frustration, and some never try again.

To avoid discouragement, some educators and coaches learn to create easy assignments. But easy assignments create an illusion of learning competence, as defects stay hidden and special talents do not surface. But when we risk failing, we expose our needs and strengths as we learn what can be improved. Stressful learning events should be sought out. They are vital to our growth.

Stress is natural and not our foe. Without the distress of hunger, we would not eat. Drinking, mating, and growing are stress-related drives. Stress itself is neutral, but attitudes about it can make or break us. Regrettably, some learners never reach their stress point. They fear the test, expect to fail, and if given a chance to flee, they'll take it every time. For others, the opposite is true: they embrace the challenge and delight in the thrill of performing at their edge.

71

They keep improving themselves and become our stars and champions. It's not that they don't fear failure. They have learned to sustain clarity and flow in crisis. And that's the point.

Stress-point education uses challenges to reveal and remedy negative learning patterns. As students strive to complete an exercise that requires several attempts, their emotional and perceptual/motor deportment is challenged and becomes the subject matter for the lesson. With each success, more difficult tasks are assigned. Each new lesson is chosen to develop new habits and skills in order to eliminate specific learning difficulties, and this process broadens the learner's experience. As harder assignments are completed, awareness sharpens and ability grows. When precision becomes a reflex, learning deficits vanish. Learners who only practice what they can easily accomplish never learn what is needed to move on.

The idea here is to hold the student to a task until a "flow state" is achieved. The strategy is to activate the flow state, strengthen it, prolong it, and then work out the disabilities. There is no failure, only feedback. In this open flow state, breakthrough learning and new brain connections occur more easily. Students expand into new skills as a unified whole rather than by closing down self-discovery and adding just another splinter skill.

In a more aware state of consciousness, students rise to the occasion, give up old patterns, release conscious control, and flow through the experience from beginning to end. In flow, the voice becomes fuller, confident, and precisely on beat. The eyes, face, and body appear intelligent and aligned with present action when golfers are in a flow state.

It seems to me that the adviser or guide's job is to carefully choose the tasks that help students attain and increase flow strength, firing neurons in the brain. With a success-oriented, nonjudgmental attitude, the coach as adviser guides the student's behavior. But the coach and learner draw environmental maps and devise shot blueprints together. As learning patterns become clear, students learn to confront their problems enthusiastically and objectively. This requires self-understanding, embracing potential imperfections with a sense of core knowledge, and playing without self-criticism.

There are people who have a real sense of wonder and will think about what others simply accept. This sense of "what if?" is a gift and the foundation for long-term learning and living a full life. A sense of wonder and "what if?" thinking are very useful when it comes to making progress. How's your sense of wonder? Did you lose it among all the how-to advice you received along the way? How-to instructions are actually a hope that advice will work. On the other hand, faith in self-learning is being open to accepting outcomes without judgments.

72

When a golfer is allowed to interact with a "what if?" approach, he or she lets go and goes with the flow of the shot at hand. This is like realizing that swimming requires letting go of the side of the pool or someone's hand. Swimmers must put faith in their own ability to use their natural buoyancy and float on the water. Golfers must have faith in self-learning and the principles of motion before any real long-term progress is achieved.

The goal of such training is to enable the student to transfer flow-state learning to any new undertaking, on or off the golf course. When students are guided to break tasks into flow-sized modules, they're on the road to achieving mastery. With this approach, improved learning capacities and habits are integrated into the functional organization of the brain beyond the training environment. In the end, perception expands, self-awareness grows, and strain and fear decrease. The individual becomes more creative, confident, and capable of navigating toward a higher-quality success.

We do not learn to play. We clearly must play to learn, and eventually to win.

We Are Educators of Whole Human Beings

Jane Tompkins

What I am asking for is a more holistic approach to learning, a disciplinary training for people who teach in college that takes into account the fact that we are educators of whole human beings, a form of higher education that would take responsibility for the emergence of an integrated person. . . .

One way of making education more holistic is to get outside the classroom and off the campus. It interrupts the programming twelve years of classroom conditioning automatically calls up; the change in environment changes everything. The class becomes a social unit; students become more fully rounded human beings—not just people who either know the answer or don't know it. Inside the classroom, it's one kind of student that dominates; outside, it's another. Qualities besides critical thinking can come to light: generosity, steadfastness, determination, practical competence, humor, ingenuity, imagination. Tying course content to the world outside offers a real-world site for asking theoretical questions; it answers students' need to feel that their education is good for something other than a grade point average. . . .

All the same, while speaking about the advantages of moving the classroom off campus, I'm troubled by the memory of my own college days. I loved college, and the main reason I loved it had to do with being in a cloistered atmosphere. Without knowing it, I chose a small liberal arts college for women located in an affluent suburb because it did not ask me to cope with too many new things at once.

It was intellectual achievement above everything at Bryn Mawr, and I identified with that. . . . But now I wish that the college I bound my identity over to had introduced me to my heart. I wish it had set mercy and compassion before me as idols, instead of Athena's cold brow. I wish I had been encouraged to look inward, been guided on a quest for understanding my own turmoil, self-doubts, fears. How much pain it might have saved me later on.

This was a use for the cloister: to screen out the world and enable the gaze to turn inward in contemplation. For the growth of human beings an environment set apart and protected from the world is essential. But the cloister needs to be used for the purposes for which it was originally intended: quiet reflection, self-observation, meditative awareness. These are gifts of the cloister that allow the heart to open without fear.

Most institutions of higher learning in our country do not address the inner lives of their students, except as a therapeutic stopgap. To get help with your self you have to go to a clinic and be assigned a psychiatric counselor to help you with your problem, or, if you are a member of a mainstream religious denomination, you can go to its representative in the campus ministries. As far as the university is concerned, the core of the human being, his or her emotional and spiritual life, is dealt with as a necessary evil, on the sidelines, and the less heard about it the better. We don't want people to think of our students as having problems. But having a problem with your self is the existential dilemma, the human condition. Learning to deal with our own suffering is the beginning of wisdom. . . .

The curriculum of American education, kindergarten through graduate school, is externally oriented. Even psychology and religion are externalized bodies of knowledge, with terminologies and methodologies and histories to be mastered like anything else. Every freshman can tell you that Socrates said, "Know thyself," but is she or he then given any way to carry out the charge? Undergraduates, you may say, are preoccupied with nothing but themselves. They are self-absorbed to a fault. Perhaps, but their self-preoccupation is a function of the stage of life they're at; they want to ask the big existential questions, and they want to know themselves in the Socratic sense. But instead of giving them the means, or the incentive, our present system sidelines this hugely important phase of human development and relegates it to the dormitory. Whoever wants to know herself is strictly on her own.

Occasionally in a literature class, or a women's studies class, undergraduates will be asked to write or speak from their own experience. Often they do so passionately, eloquently. But this is a kind of exception practiced in the corners of humanities departments and is widely regarded as "soft," unrigorous, not a substitute for history, methodology, theory, terminology, information. And of course it's not a substitute; it's simply knowledge of a different kind, but of a kind that, although essential to the conduct of every single human life, has practically no standing in our curricula.

I am not advocating a curriculum devoted exclusively to the pursuit of self-knowledge. I too well remember the rapture of my undergraduate days in the east wing of the Bryn Mawr library reading the thirteenth-century Italian poets. I loved the voyage out. It was full of wonder and excitement. But in order to have a balanced, nonobsessive relation to the world outside yourself, some inner balance and self-understanding are needed. Otherwise, your engagement with the world sooner or later becomes captive to the claims of obscure actors to whom you are paying hush money behind your own back. The old unmet demons—anger, fear, self-hatred, envy, you name it—end up running the show,

We Are Educators of Whole Human Beings

under the guise of doing sociolinguistics, or molecular biology, or tax litigation, or child advocacy, or *ikebana*, or whatever it happens to be.

Inside and outside, the cloister and the world. We need both. But somehow higher learning has evolved to a point where it offers neither. Neither contact with the world nor contact with ourselves. This has come about because the university has relinquished responsibility for envisioning life as a whole. Instead, it has become an umbrella organization under which a variety of activities go on, but one that has no center and no soul. Correspondingly, the university doesn't see the student as a whole person but only as a kind of cutout part of a person, the intellect—a segment that it services diligently.

I don't know how to bring into being the world I'm trying to imagine here. I can't imagine it, really. All I can imagine are the kinds of adjustments I suggested in a report I made to the deans, such as introducing more experience-based courses into the curriculum, finding ways to de-emphasize grades, deepening the role of advisors, educating parents about the purpose of a liberal arts education.

In fact, I'm afraid to envision the kind of world my experience has taught me to reach for, because I fear it would seem too outlandish, impossible. I don't think most of us ever try to imagine our ideal world as educators. We're not encouraged to, certainly. I have taught in colleges and universities for thirty years, but no one has ever said to me, "Tompkins, have your vision of an ideal university on my desk by tomorrow morning." When did anybody ever say that?

Higher education, in order to produce the knowledge and skills students need to enter certain lucrative professions, cuts students off both from their inner selves and from the world around them. By not offering them a chance to know themselves and come into contact with the actual social environment, it prepares them to enter professional schools but not to develop as whole human beings. Although parents might object—What, all that tuition and no ticket to financial security and social success?—it would be more helpful to students if, as a starting point, universities conceived education less as training for a career than as the introduction to a life.

Jane Tompkins

Part Two

II. Stances and Strategies: Teaching as a Balancing Act

Don't Dance with Wolves

Jackie Wilcox

Because of incomplete credit transfers, I took many of the undergraduate education classes twice, fifteen years apart, first in Britain, then in the United States. In both countries I learned all the educationally correct theories about how students should be regarded as individuals, all having different learning styles, and so on. However, in neither country was I ever taught how to quiet and subdue a class of thirty teenagers with raging hormones, forced against their natural instincts to sit in uncomfortable chairs, long enough for them to learn anything, in any style. I did ask the education professors, "What about discipline?" and got much the same answer in both countries: "If you motivate them to learn, they will pay attention." It seems to me that is putting the cart before the horse. In any case, by the time I began teaching senior undergraduates the "Methods of Teaching English in High School" course, I had spent fifteen years in some pretty tough classrooms.

I would start thus: "Despite what you have learned in education classes about children being individuals, the truth is that a class of thirty students is a wolf pack. You have to decide whether you are going to be the Alpha wolf or dinner." Now, this statement, of course, was designed to shock my students into attention (more about that later). But I still think this is not a bad metaphor, and it applies to all classes, from kindergarten to graduate school, but particularly to teenagers. An average class will give a new teacher about a twenty-minute grace period before it attacks. Want more details? Read any book on pack behavior.

If educating is a process of leading to knowledge, teachers have to learn to lead. This means they must earn the respect of the pack, not assume they have it automatically because they signed a contract with the university or the education authority. You don't get respect by trying to be pals, buddies, friends with your students: you get contempt; they will smirk and mark you as a loser or an easy mark. You don't get respect by being a sex symbol of either sex, though you might get initial attention. You don't get respect by appealing to students' better natures; as a pack, they don't have one, though individually they may be angelic. And whatever you do, don't try to fake it. Students can smell a fake as he or she walks into the classroom—and you won't be able to keep it up. So how do you walk into a classroom—any classroom—and establish immediate authority? Get in sync with yourself, find your style, customize it, and tell jokes. This was my experience.

I was named Jacqueline after my grandmother, but no matter what school I went to (and my parents moved a lot) or how I fought, I was always called Jackie. Jacquelines are cool, quiet, and elegant; Jackies are loud, brash, and slightly vulgar. When I was fifteen, Mrs. Davis, my English teacher, was my ideal. She was soft voiced, composed, always prepared, in control, beautifully dressed, and we knew she had to be wearing lingerie with real lace. This was the image I aimed at when I became a teacher myself. It didn't work of course; I couldn't even afford the lingerie. I was probably thirty before I realized that I would never become Mrs. Davis, that I would never be a Jacqueline, and that it didn't matter. I am loud and brash and occasionally vulgar. I get excited and I wave my hands (and other body parts) around a lot. On the other hand, in a different way, my students learn from me as much as I did from Mrs. Davis. I can communicate my enthusiasm for what I teach in a way that Mrs. Davis really didn't; that somehow makes up for my losing my place, my cool, and the occasional paper. So learn your strengths and use them.

All this has something to do with getting older and not caring about it, or leaving your egocentric self-consciousness at home. If you are afraid of looking like a fool, you will look a fool. The first step in losing self-consciousness is in appearance. My teenage years were bad: I never really felt clean, and sweaty embarrassment, acne, and puppy fat, whether real or imagined, hurt. When I was a new teacher in my twenties, it was even more difficult. I couldn't hide in the bathroom when the class of thirty was waiting with sixty beady little eyes focused on critical inspection.

Looking professional will give you confidence. I once taught a "methods" class where we had a discussion on professional appearance. The students came up with the usual: use deodorant and breath mints, and if you have a short skirt, don't raise your arms or bend, but one student told of a teacher she had had who would sit on the edge of her desk, with her very hairy, unshaven legs at eye level. Other students tried to think of worse offenses, but the consensus was that there weren't any. As I have aged, I have become less concerned about what students think of my physical appearance or clothes, but I have found a style of my own that is professional without being obtrusive or distracting, and I always shave my legs.

The other thing you have to forget when teaching is fear, and fear comes in many guises. Never be afraid of losing your job; if you are smart enough to be a teacher you already know that there are many better-paying, easier jobs out there (my dental hygienist has a B.Ed., Bill Cosby began as a teacher, and so did Stephen King). They need us more than we need them. This attitude gives you a moral freedom.

Don't be afraid of deviating from your lesson plans. One of my best lessons was with a class of fifteen-year-olds. I think we were reading *The Crucible*. It had been raining, but the sun came out and the most incredible double rainbow flooded the classroom with color. So I called time-out and we all went to the window to watch while it lasted. One boy asked me how the rainbows were formed. I had to admit I didn't know (never be afraid to admit ignorance), but I dragged the physics teacher out of his planning time in the faculty lounge and he explained. This led to a week of combined Physics/English lessons in which the students were passionately interested. I can't remember what happened to *The Crucible*.

After learning to lead and conquering fear, you need to be aware of and avoid the "teacher syndromes." These are not diseases, though they have symptoms, and they affect people in different ways. The obvious examples are the elementary school teachers who speak to and treat everyone as though they are second graders, the English teachers who correct their acquaintances' grammar, and anyone who talks down to the most important person in educational establishments, the janitor. When you are paid for x hours a week to be the expert in a certain area, it can become habit-forming, and you can become arrogant. The best defense against teacher syndrome is to cultivate humility, realize how much you are learning from your students in areas that are not your expertise, and think jokes.

Why jokes? Verbal humor is what distinguishes man from animal. It takes a certain level of intelligence to appreciate verbal humor. It kick-starts the brain (when I get up, I always read the comics before attempting the front page). Once the students accept you as their leader, you can relax. They are with you. You can begin to treat them as human beings, equals who have not been alive as long, so are less knowledgeable, though not less smart. Now it is your job to take their brains into new territory. Go for it. Lead the pack and make them think. It may be for the first time in their lives, and they may find they like it and surprise you. Because you have the framework of leadership established and you have lost your fear and self-consciousness, you are now in a position to foster those who are different without losing face, to encourage the nerds and give them authenticity. Little by little, you can change the world.

83

Teaching from Behind

Michael L. Keene

The odd bits of pedagogical instruction I received as a new teaching assistant in an English department in the early 1970s never made much sense to me—at best they were inadequate, and at worst they were hopelessly elitist and visibly ineffective. Basically, one was expected to show students well-written essays (by John Stuart Mill, George Orwell, and other dead white men), talk with the students about the essays, and then give the students assignments to write their own essays—presumably equally timeless. The system presupposed that the students, having more or less passively analyzed the elements of a well-written essay, could then go out and write their own. Most of the students did a pretty poor job, and their grades reflected it. As I see things today, that approach is about like teaching a dog to fetch a stick by throwing the stick and then kicking the dog if the dog fails to retrieve it.

About the same time I started teaching writing, I also started teaching for the Red Cross—swimming, sailing, and canoeing. The Red Cross's philosophy of teaching started with establishing trust between the students and the teacher, and it paid lots of attention to timing—when are the students ready to hear about a particular skill, when are they ready to see it demonstrated, and when are they ready to try it out for themselves? Along the way, the teacher demonstrated the particular skill (not coincidentally showing that he or she in fact *had* the skill), and as soon as possible the students were involved in trying out the skill themselves. The pedagogy was (and is) very much small step by small step, very much interactive, and very much hands-on. Generally, the sooner the students got to the hands-on part, the better things went. That approach made sense to me instantly. Thirty-plus years later, it still makes sense.

My philosophy is that students don't learn from what the teacher does, students learn from what the teacher has the students do. Just as you can't teach a student to paddle a canoe in a straight line by keeping the student on shore listening to lectures, you can't teach writing unless the students themselves get directly involved in the messy business that goes into it, learning firsthand the various skills, tricks, and bits of understanding requisite to the activity. Ultimately, it doesn't do much good for me to show the students films and pictures of people paddling canoes in a straight line; the students need to paddle the canoes themselves.

The courses I teach are all writing courses, mostly either technical writing or a dissertation-writing course. Students take these courses for very utilitarian reasons, reasons that would make it easy for me to use a totally directive pedagogy if I chose to do so. Because the students have very immediate and practical goals coming into these courses (to satisfy a curriculum requirement, to finish a dissertation), it's easy to hold their attention with lectures. Many of these students like it when I tell them step by step, inch by inch, exactly what to write. And I could. I *could* tell students point by point, both in theoretical terms and in very practical terms, exactly what needs to go into writing, for example, a good proposal. I could cover the process logically; use examples to analyze every section, heading, and line critically; and tell the students exactly what questions usually come up and how those questions should be dealt with. After thirty years in the classroom, I can lecture on such things pretty well, and in the process I can have the students rapt with interest, chuckling with wry humor, or sad about the injustices of the power relationships inherent in the world of proposal writing and "big science." And in the cases of the very *best* students, anyway, this approach *could* produce good proposals, if by "good proposals" one means proposals that exactly mirror whatever I said in my lecture.

If what I wanted to produce was only one very good proposal, one very good job-application letter, one very good methodology section, or one very good literature review, maybe that "sage on a stage" approach would suffice.

But my goal in fact is to produce better writers (where "better" means, among other things, more able to handle the many various demands professional life and/or graduate school will put on their writing abilities), rather than to produce just one better piece of writing (where "better" means "exactly per the terms of Mike's lectures"). "Better writers" for me also means people who may even come to find some pleasure in their writing, people who for that reason may be drawn back to their writing, to doing more writing, and especially to continuing to grow and change (both as writers and as human beings) because of the capabilities their writing gives them. Measured by the goal of producing better writers, those wonderful lectures—and that pedagogical approach—fall short by a considerable distance.

Today in my teaching I try to create situations in which I have given students all the pieces they need to learn something new (whether those "pieces" are skills, knowledge, or ways of understanding), and then I create an assignment through which the students go out and learn to apply those pieces on their own. Every writing assignment starts with planning and with rough drafts. Either I review the students' rough drafts, or the students work in groups to review each other's rough drafts under my supervision. Then the students go through another learning cycle by revising those drafts, and then they submit final copies to me. Often I return the final copies with notes for more revision. At the end of the semester, students rework most of their earlier assignments one more time into a final document to submit to me.

With some students, this student-centered approach is sometimes less popular; these are the students who say, "Just tell me exactly what it is you want to hear." But I find it's much more effective pedagogy to accomplish my goal of producing better writers. It makes the students much more responsible for their own learning, with me as a resource most often following along just a step or two behind them. It encourages the students to develop the kinds of lifelong learning skills they will all need.

One name for this approach is "leading from behind." The phrase is used in the *Tao Tê Ching*, in the education literature, and in sailboat racing (where I learned it). For me it means that my students learn best when I'm not out in front of them but right beside them (or even a short step behind them). The students do not learn from what I say (or not very much, anyway) or from what I do (or not directly, anyway); the students learn from what I have the students do.

To do an effective job of teaching from behind, you have to know as much as you can about your students. People who address anonymous audiences often feel (whether they know it or not) a really strong tendency to lecture. Perhaps that's because if you don't know the people you're dealing with, it's natural to be a little bit afraid of what they might say or do if given the chance to say or do something. (This may be the way most of us started out, as beginning teachers in graduate school—and too few of us get around to changing it. More on that later.) Thus the lecturer tendency most of us share is fed by not knowing much about our students.

Who are these people who sit in front of you three hours a week? What kinds of backgrounds do they come from in general, and in particular (if it's a writing course) what is their background as writers? Why are they in the course you're teaching (is it a requirement or an elective)? What do they hope to get out of it (just a grade, be it an A or a C; or do they want to learn something they actually see themselves using after the course is ended)? You just about have to get answers to these questions for each new group of students you teach. If you do the work to discover this information, you'll find teaching from behind is an easier position to take than it might otherwise be. You might also find your feelings about teaching tend to stay fresh and new longer because you see in front of you not the same featureless sea of faces from term to term, but very different groups of very different individuals, like the patterns in a kaleidoscope if someone were continually changing the colored objects in front of its lens.

A particularly good way to learn about your students is to pay attention to the questions they ask—detailed, specific attention. It's so tempting, especially if you teach the same courses over and over again, to hear the first three or four words out of a student's mouth and jump in with the answer because you figure (if you were to stop and do any figuring) you've heard the question a hundred or a thousand times before.

Stepping on the student's question by premature answering may prove to you what a clever person you are, but it does not do much for the student's learning. The student who asks that question hasn't asked it a hundred times before or heard your answer a hundred times before, so there's a nice little micro-learning process going on that you can either squelch by premature answering or nourish by clamping your mouth shut (except to make noises like "uh-huh" or "I'm with you, keep going with this" or some such) until the question is finished, then paraphrasing the question back to the student to make sure you're both pursuing the same point ("Let me see if I understand what you're asking: you want to know . . . , is that right?") and, only after all that, coming up with your answer.

Another way to improve your focus on your students is to ask yourself, for each class meeting and each assignment, who it is among the students you are focusing on. For example, are you paying particular attention to the students in the class who are struggling the most or to those in the middle or to those who are already doing the best? Too much of the time, we all tend to teach to a more or less mythical common denominator in our classes, and that can be another symptom of not knowing enough about our students in detail. If you focus your teaching each day on just one skill level or knowledge level in your class, you move each individual group (and eventually the whole class) more effectively in the direction(s) you want them to go.

A final way to listen to and learn from your students is to have the students do evaluations of your courses and your teaching, and then for you to pay attention to those evaluations. At the very least, you need to have a formal mechanism set up (be it as anonymous as a questionnaire or as personal as individual office interviews) through which you get feedback from your students on your course and your teaching. Especially early in my career, and even today if I am teaching a new course, I like to ask students to do both a midterm and a final evaluation. Even if the evaluation is only some standard form on which students fill in little bubbles and then a computer reports a score to you, you can learn from the experience. And if you can have students simply write a paragraph about your course and your teaching in addition to the form, you can learn much more. If you are fortunate enough to be able to do one-to-one interviews with the students, you can really change your behavior based on that valuable feedback.

Of course you read or listen to these responses critically. The student who says "I wish we had class outside more often" is not going to lead me to take the class outside more, but she may cause me to wonder what it is that's going on inside the classroom that's driving that request. Perhaps it's as simple as the room being too hot. Or maybe I need to suggest the students get their desks out of the rows and into a circle, or to move them into clusters as they do when they're working in their peer review groups.

One of the important moments in my making the decision to try to lead from behind in my teaching (and in starting to figure out how to do it) was when I decided to end my dissertation-writing class with exit interviews with each student. All I had to do was to start asking, "Are there topics you wish we had covered in this class that we didn't cover—what are they?" and "Are there topics we covered, or things we did, in this class that you thought we spent too much time on—if so, what are they?" and the students themselves started telling me the directions they needed to go in—and pretty much exactly what I needed to do to help them get there.

Besides listening carefully to their students, teachers who want to lead from behind also need to keep triangulating what they are doing against how other people in other settings are going about their own teaching. If you want to lecture all the time, paying attention to others' teaching may not matter so much. But if you want to be versatile enough to move your students in particular ways without (metaphorically) dragging them there, you've got to keep checking on your own positioning—relative to the class, to the discipline you're teaching, to your own pedagogical approach. Listening to your students, as presented earlier in this essay, suggests one set of ways to do that. Hearing what's going on in your own teaching offers another set of ways.

Studying the ways other teachers work in the classroom is especially important on the college level, where most teaching is essentially a solitary activity: once I go into a classroom and close the door, no one in my department, much less the rest of the university, knows what it is I'm doing—not the people in the classrooms next to mine, not my best friends in the department. Usually I'm in there alone with the students. But to continue to grow as a teacher I simply must see what other teachers are doing. If you are early enough in your career that you are still taking coursework, or if you are just the kind of person who continues to take courses anyway (whether in making pottery or reading medieval history), you can study what the teachers in those other courses are doing and learn from their activities.

Another easy way to become informed about other teachers' teaching is to read about teaching. Early in my career I read Ken Macrorie's *A Vulnerable Teacher* (Hayden Book Company, 1974), and it planted a seed in my mind back in 1975 that in fact was the beginning of this whole "leading from behind" approach for me. Donald Murray's *A Writer Teaches Writing* (Houghton Mifflin,

1968), which I discovered only after reading the Macrorie book, showed me ways to implement the approach Macrorie's book suggested. Today there are plenty of good books about teaching, from quasi-scientific studies to personal narratives, and if teaching is important enough to you to make a living at it, teaching should be important enough to you to read about how other people do it. In my field, the ongoing editions of Edward P. J. Corbett, Nancy Myers, and Gary Tate's *The Writing Teacher's Sourcebook* (currently in its 4th edition; Oxford University Press, 2000) help me hear a multiplicity of voices speaking about the different ways people teach and learn writing.

A third way to study other teachers is to put yourself into team teaching situations. Where I teach, this is difficult because the institution offers no way for two people to receive credit for teaching one class. Even so, there are plenty of ways to place yourself into the same classroom with another teacher—by guest appearances in other teachers' classes, by coteaching in volunteer situations (in my case, at my church, but it could just as easily be teaching swimming for the Red Cross), or (as I do) by doing workshops together with other teachers at professional meetings. The more I can see and hear and be present for the ways other people work in classrooms, the better I will be at my work in the classroom.

Just as teaching with other teachers can be instructive, so can teaching other students in other settings. One of my best friends has taught at the junior high, high school, junior college, and now major research university levels, and I have always thought that abundance of experience with different students in different settings makes him a much better teacher. For me, I was fortunate to spend many summers working with ten-to-fourteen-year-olds, teaching swimming, sailing, and canoeing. And now I lead classes at church for aging Baby Boomers like myself.

All of those experiences, although valuable and rewarding in and of themselves, are like teaching laboratories for me. Because those settings, students, and subjects are so different from the ones I deal with at the university, they make it easier for me to reflect on what I do at the university, giving me a perspective that, at least sometimes, allows me to make good changes in what I do at the university. If I only knew one way to do what I do, I would be a much poorer teacher. But at this point in my career I want to be able to have lots of options, and I develop those options through reflecting on my experiences in these other settings.

The critical change in my teaching that resulted when I began to do exit interviews with students is but one example of the many ways my teaching has changed over the thirty or so years I've taught. For all career teachers, at some point the question becomes, "What will you do next?" If you do not find a way to continue to grow and change as a teacher, what do you suppose your fifteenth, or twentieth, or twenty-fifth year will be like? In particular, what habits do you have today as a teacher—such as lecturing—that you may have begun at the very start of your career, when you didn't know your students or your subject very well, or when you were afraid to try a pedagogy that might be a little risky? Isn't it time to adjust the way you teach today to what you know today?

However good you may already be in the classroom, a compelling reason to continue to improve and to change in important ways comes from the sheer longevity of careers today. As I write this today I am fifty-four years old, with thirty-one years of teaching behind me and perhaps another ten or fifteen in front of me. Either I find ways to make what I do seem fresh and challenging— if only to me, but I hope also to my students—or I face a really grim, same dull grind over and over for another thirty semesters. Perhaps because I started out so totally devoted to lecturing, to the exclusion of nearly anything else, I find the concept of learning how to lead from behind in the classroom powerfully attractive. The benefits for the students are tangible, but my interest here is also in the benefits for me. Because I learn more about my students and about the classes I teach, they are new to me each term.

This teaching philosophy puts the students out in front of me in important ways. While I'm never far behind, and certainly I'm still expressing a certain subtle control over the general direction things are going, I am not *leading* in any conventional sense of the word. The payoff for such teaching is that the students have a lot more of a voice in where they go than might otherwise be the case, and because their own investment in their learning is correspondingly increased— the struggle is theirs, the writing is theirs, and the learning is theirs—their learning is increased as well.

If I am successful in this pedagogy, students will understand what I'm talking about when I end the semester with this quote from poet William Stafford:

> Writers may not be special—sensitive or talented— in any usual sense. They are simply engaged in sustained use of a language skill we all have. Their "creations" come about through confident reliance on stray impulses that will, with trust, find occasional patterns that are satisfying. But writing itself is one of the great, free human activities. There is scope for individuality, and elation, and discovery in writing. For the person who follows with trust and forgiveness what occurs to him, the world remains always ready and deep, an inexhaustible environment, with the combined vividness

91

of an actuality and flexibility of a dream. Working back and forth between experience and thought, writers have more than space and time can offer. They have the whole unexplored realm of human vision.

At the end of a really good semester, I might follow that quote with this one from Anne Lamott, and, again, if I've done my job, the students understand how the quote and the class are connected:

> "So why does our writing matter, again?" they [her writing students] ask. "Because of the spirit," I say. "Because of the heart. Writing and reading decrease our sense of isolation. They deepen and widen and expand our sense of life; they feed the soul. When writers make us shake our heads with the exactness of their prose and their truths, and even make us laugh about ourselves, our life, our buoyancy is restored. We are given a shot at dancing with, or at least clapping along with, the absurdity of life, instead of being squashed by it over and over again. It's like singing on a boat during a terrible storm at sea. You can't stop the raging storm, but singing can change the hearts and spirits of the people who are together on that ship."

The Art of Motivating Students

Gayle M. Seymour

In her 1635 *Self-Portrait as the Allegory of Painting* (Royal Collection, Windsor Castle), the Italian Baroque artist Artemisia Gentileschi depicted herself, paintbrush in hand, in the act of painting. Her wild hair intimates the intensity of the creative process; the iridescent fabric of her dress demonstrates the painter's skill in handling color; and around her neck hangs a mask pendant, emblematic of the artist's ability to imitate the human face just as painting imitates nature. But it is the gold chain on which the pendant hangs that holds the most significance because, according to sixteenth-century emblemographer Cesare Ripa, it symbolizes "the continuity and interlocking nature of painting, each man learning from his master and continuing his master's achievements in the next generation." Thus Gentileschi proudly pays tribute to her teacher, her father Orazio Gentileschi, who taught her to paint.

My decision to become a teacher and art historian can be linked, as in the iconography of Gentileschi's gold chain, to the influence of a great teacher I had in college, Dr. Henri Dorra. Although I sat in his classroom for the first time over twenty-five years ago, I can still remember the overwhelming sensation of excitement I felt when he lectured on such paintings as Renoir's *Luncheon of the Boating Party* (1880, Phillips Collection, Washington, D.C.). While other students may have found a darkened classroom and slides an irresistible opportunity to take a nap, I found myself totally transported to another world by Dr. Dorra's lectures. In his passionate discussion of a painting's sheer beauty or of an artist's ability to handle complex ideas in mere paint and canvas, my teacher was somehow able to create moments of revelation for his students; by viewing just one glorious painting, we had somehow seen them all. I can remember leaving his classroom with feelings of fullness and satisfaction, the way one feels after enjoying a superb meal. Although my Dr. Dorra has retired, his enthusiasm for art lives on through me and in my students as well. My goal in teaching is to kindle that spark of excitement in my students, just as my teacher had done in me, so that art would become not just a profession but a passion. But this is easier said than done. The trick is finding just the right hook that will cause students to connect actively with their discipline, to experience the participatory excitement of discovery, and to understand that the learning process extends beyond the classroom. I have found that what works best in motivating students is an activity that they typically seem to dread—research. I'm not talking about assigning a paper topic and sending students off to the library, although that method certainly has its place in teaching. What I'm suggesting is research that connects the classroom to the real world. Allow me to explain this idea by offering two examples of research projects in which my students have been passionately involved.

I teach a course on public art that prominently features field research in major urban centers. For many rural-Arkansas students who have been raised in geographically and culturally isolated communities, it is quite possible that they have never actually seen an original work of art. My idea was to get students to conduct research on public sculpture they would actually be able to see and then provide them with opportunities to continue their research on site, either through archival/library research or by interviewing professionals in the field. The most difficult part of coordinating field research like this is getting students to see your vision and motivating them enough to work toward completion of the research, no matter what it takes. My students were so excited about the possibility of a six-day road trip that they hardly noticed that I had said the word "research"; neither did they complain when I told them they were going to write the grants to fund their research. Sometimes you just have to be sneaky in motivating students. I try to take advantage of every step of the process to get students to commit themselves to their project. The activity of writing the grant, for instance, caused my students to take ownership of their research and to see it as something important and worthwhile.

My fifteen students were successful in obtaining their grants, and they did carry out research on public art in Washington, D.C. Enough preliminary research was done before the trip that when we arrived at the various sculpture sites my students were absolutely giddy about seeing what, by now, had become "old friends." As we stood in front of Maya Lin's Vietnam Veterans Memorial (1981–83, The Mall) or Nancy Holt's *Dark Star Park* (1984, Rosslyn, Virginia), for instance, my students were able to lecture on their particular monuments to the rest of the group. These were moments of transformation—they had become the experts! Our trip, incidentally, coincided with an international symposium on public art sponsored by the Smithsonian's Save Outdoor Sculpture! (SOS!) project, which provided the perfect resource—artists, conservators, arts administrators, and teachers from all over the world—for my students' research. "I couldn't believe I was actually meeting and speaking to [public sculptor] Luis Jimenez," remarked my student Robert. Through this experience these students became active learners, engaged in their research alongside other professionals. Another student, Traci, summarized her experience: "The SOS! Conference left me with a sense of confidence in myself and my education. It is one thing to study art from a classroom, but it is quite another thing to interact with the art world." These same students went back into their own communities recognizing the intentions and value of—or absence of—local outdoor sculpture.

Topics such as public art allow my students to use the world as part of their classroom; however, the classroom also allows my students to be part of the world. On the first day of my senior seminar in 1997 I announced that, in addition to studying the history of the mural, we were going to go out into the community and actually make one. "It really sounded crazy," remembered student Bethann, "and looking back now, I don't quite know how we did it, but it was one of the best experiences of my life." My eleven students ended up collaborating with over four hundred local ninth-grade physical science students to create a fifteen-by-forty-five-foot mural, *Essential Elements*, for the courtyard of Conway High School's new science building.

Motivating students is always the hardest part of any group project. You have to get them to see that the process is as important as the product and that the work involved is not done just to get a grade but for some greater good. Once my students understood that the mural was not about them but about the ninth-grade community at the high school, they were able to commit themselves to completing the project. My job was not to be a dictator but a facilitator and coach. I knew that if I taught by example—working alongside my students, spending the same long hours they were spending, evenings and weekends—they would be right there with me to get the job done. Instead of a traditional mural painted on a wall, these students devised an ingenious method of painting onto cutout shapes of treated plywood that could be screwed into the wall, thus eliminating the need for scaffolding or working in a linear fashion. This method of using portable sections also allowed physically challenged students to work alongside their more able-bodied classmates. In the end, my students learned powerful lessons about the history of the mural outside those normally found in a textbook. They realized that public art is not just about aesthetic decisions but involves complex logistical, bureaucratic, and economic decisions. By encouraging new ideas and approaches to the art of the mural, these students were motivated to work collaboratively in a joint intellectual effort, to create art that touches real life. More than anything, they realized that art is a powerful connector that can create community identity; that public art can serve as a source of community pride; and that we all have a responsibility to give back to our own communities.

Connecting the classroom to the real world is my way of showing students that research can be fun and that learning is dynamic, exciting, and filled with the unexpected. Whether students are conducting field research, attending

Gayle M. Seymour

conferences, or even creating a community mural, the point is that these experiences do change students' outlooks or sensibilities about their world and, more important, their places in it. I can only hope that someday my students' passion for art will infect their own students or coworkers. Only a few weeks ago I received a telephone call from one of those students who had worked on the mural. She was calling to tell me she had gotten a job teaching eleventh-grade English and that she was going to have her kids paint a mural! In moments like that, I reflect on the influence Dr. Dorra has had on my life and how his passion for art still lives on in my students. I am reminded of Nicolas Poussin's great painting *Blind Orion Searching for the Rising Sun* (1658, Metropolitan Museum of Art, New York), which depicts a giant supporting a small figure on his shoulders. Ideologically, it represents my concept of the interlocking nature of teaching, that those of us who teach owe a great debt to our predecessors, but we must see even farther when we are mounted on their shoulders.

And the Oscar Goes to . . .

Thomas W. Woolley Jr.

One of my most enduring preschool memories from the late 1950s is of afternoon rides with my mom in an old Chevy to pick up my dad from work. I would always run down the long open corridors to my dad's room. I was afraid to touch the human skeleton hanging just inside the door, and the animal organs preserved in jars were just plain gross. What remains with me most vividly, however, is the pithy odor of formaldehyde. My dad was a high school biology and physiology teacher. I knew what a teacher was; after all, when my mom went to her part-time job as a secretary, I did time at Kiddie Korral and we had teachers there. My teachers were OK, but I certainly didn't want to grow up to do what my dad did—it smelled too bad.

Fifteen years later I headed to college to major in marine biology. Teaching as a career option was nowhere on the radar screen; what I did know with certainty as a seventeen-year-old was that I was destined to become the next Jacques Cousteau. Bad advice from an advisor (imagine that) in my sophomore year had me enrolled in statistics as a way to avoid taking organic chemistry. Not only did I nearly fail statistics twice, I still had to endure organic. Upon entering my master's degree program, I was informed that I would have to repeat the statistics courses that I'd suffered through during my undergraduate years. As a fallback, I decided to do whatever was necessary to get my teaching certification, since I wasn't confident that Jacques Cousteau's job would be available when I graduated. To get certified to teach I had to take certain education classes, of course, but I also had to intern in a science classroom. When I arrived for the first day of my internship in a seventh-grade science classroom, I was greeted by my junior high school homeroom teacher, who'd since moved to my college town. Having her around made me nervous enough but not nearly as uneasy as the thirty or so demons disguised as young adolescents she turned over to me every morning. It was three months of interminable chaos; surely I'd skipped some mandatory education class that outlined the secrets of successful teaching and I was now paying the price. I decided that the whole experience was a divine revelation from the god of vocations pointing me in any direction but teaching. I returned to my graduate program tired and disillusioned but with a bit more maturity and the conviction never to have children.

A wonderful statistics teacher, however, opened new doors of opportunity for me. She enthusiastically conveyed concepts and methods that had totally eluded me only a few short years before. Miraculously, she led me to a "Victor Kiam" experience. Remember those Remington razor commercials? "My wife bought me a Remington; I liked it so much that I bought the company." Well, four years later I, too, had bought the company as I received my Ph.D. in statistics. It had been during my doctoral program, earning a living as a teaching assistant, that I first enjoyed teaching. I began to think (though I would try to repress the notion) that an academic career might be more rewarding than one as an "industrial" statistician.

Looking back on twenty years of teaching experience, I now see clearly that it was my doctoral advisor, Ken Brewer, who taught me how to teach: not by formal instruction, but rather by example. He showed me that teaching is like acting; it represents an avenue of creative freedom and exploration as well as an emotional release. Like him, I tend toward introversion in social situations. (Need proof? I'm an INTJ on the Myers Briggs!) However, in front of the classroom, my stage, I have license to morph into an endless variety of alternative personalities. When I'm frustrated, I yell; when I'm impassioned, my voice winds its way through a seemingly infinite array of inflections untapped in any other arena of my life; and too often I make embarrassingly stupid jokes and puns that (fortunately) elude me outside of the classroom. This kind of freedom has allowed for continuous pedagogical experimentation ranging from the use of computer simulations to problem-based learning. Over the years, a willingness to dare to explore numerous personas in my classroom theater has opened my eyes to what I believe is the key to successful teaching and learning.

As a statistician, I am faced with teaching a subject that is not only technical in nature and universal in application but also unparalleled in evoking angst among all manner of students, undergraduate and graduate, young and old, the relatively innumerate and quantitatively proficient. All students enter the classroom for the first time with a curiosity about what will transpire over the term if not downright fear concerning their ability to succeed. Also, I am convinced that all students enter a new class with insecurity; in this regard they differ from one another only in degree. During my first visit with a class, I share my own apprehension, not only with the present situation—a new course with new students—but also latent anxieties associated with my personal struggle with college statistics. Usually the initial reaction of the students is that, if their professor spelled statistics *F-A-I-L*, then there is absolutely no hope for them. Eventually, however, the discussion meanders around to the point where they begin to understand that I've been in their seat before and maybe, just maybe, I can relate to what they are about to go through. Nothing beats establishing an atmosphere of mutual respect and trust early in the course, a sense that we're all on this intellectual journey together.

I am convinced also that students are pragmatic. The value of an informative, well-organized syllabus is too often underestimated by teachers. Most students appreciate having daily assignments outlined for the term on the syllabus, which helps them structure their time outside of class while staying focused on the core of the course content. Students assume that their teachers are subject-matter competent, though too often they do not expect, or see, genuine caring and compassion or high personal and academic expectations from their teachers. What neither students nor teachers seem to recognize is the tremendous value of enthusiasm (if not downright excitement) and humor in reducing anxiety, breaking through mental blocks, and catalyzing the learning process. If I cannot communicate my absolute fascination with statistics and the life of the mind in general, how can I possibly hope for my students to discover the world that has entranced me for over two decades?

Traditional pedagogy aside, there is no substitute for accomplished acting on the classroom stage. I am convinced that the same rapport that must evolve between an actor and his or her audience is a mandatory element in dynamic learning. The good teacher is far more than a talking head and purveyor of knowledge. Rather, day after day the teacher takes center stage in the continuous process of intellectual nurturing. There will be good days and bad, days of pure joy and serious disappointment and times when the bridge to the students' minds seems far too long to cross. However, as any dedicated actor, and teacher, who steps back onto that stage for every new performance knows, the show must go on. And so it will, with untold rewards for both teacher and student. Break a leg!

Thomas W. Woolley Jr.

Teaching as a Balancing Act: Strategies for Managing Competing Objectives

Dave Berque

As a new teacher struggling to design one of my first syllabi, I remember reading Doug Cooper's preface to the introductory computer science textbook *Oh! Pascal!* in hopes it would offer some guidance as to how I could most effectively design my course. Unfortunately for me, the preface did not start with words of wisdom but instead revealed that the author, despite his seasoning, faced as many problems as I did. Specifically, Cooper wrote: "I've received much advice [on preparing the second edition] including suggestions that it be longer, shorter, harder, easier, funnier yet more serious, with fewer and additional example programs, and problems that are simpler and more difficult to do, as well as more but less mathematically oriented. I'm pleased to report that all of these comments were found to be useful, and are incorporated in the second edition."

Something in Cooper's passage clearly resonated with me, for I have remembered it for more than a decade. When I first read it, however, I doubt I fully realized how predictive this passage would be of my journey as a teacher in the coming years. Hardly a day goes by when I do not think about some variation of Cooper's theme. Consider, for example, that in recent semesters students have suggested through course evaluations that my introductory course should have both fewer and more projects, which are both longer and shorter, and more structured yet more open-ended. At the same time I have been advised to do more and less group work during class, and to spend more time answering student questions while simultaneously not "wasting" as much time doing so. And, of course, there has probably never been a semester when several students did not suggest that the course should move faster, while several others proclaimed that I was covering material too rapidly.

Advice from faculty colleagues may follow a similar contradictory pattern. For example, one's colleagues may suggest that teaching effectiveness can be enhanced by being more supportive of students or by challenging them more, by asking insightful questions or revealing profound answers, by reinforcing the viewpoints of a textbook author or offering contradictory opinions to balance those views, and by staying quieter during class discussions or interjecting more forcefully at key points to refocus the group.

Of course, teachers are not the only professionals who must consider competing approaches to accomplishing their goals. For example, in his book *Invention by Design: How Engineers Get from Thought to Thing* Henry Petroski provides a glimpse into the way engineers resolve design challenges by presenting a series of case studies that describe the history of the design of objects ranging from the low-tech paper-clip to the high-tech fax machine. Petroski's case studies illustrate how social, political, aesthetic, environmental, economic, and many other factors play a role in design and how considering these factors often suggest competing approaches that the engineer must balance. One of the overarching themes emerging from these case studies is best summarized by Petroski when he writes, "All design involves conflicting objectives and hence compromise, and the best designs will always be those that come up with the best compromise." When I first read this passage, and all of Petroski's supporting evidence, I was reminded of the preface to *Oh! Pascal!* It has become my firm belief that the process of designing a good textbook, syllabus, or classroom activity is similar to the process of designing a more traditional object; each requires the designer to carefully resolve conflicting objectives.

How does an effective teacher determine how to resolve such conflicts? While there are almost certainly no silver bullets or magic formulas to help answer this question, or at least none that I am aware of, I believe there are two underlying guidelines that, if followed, will increase the likelihood that a teacher will make the right compromises. The first guideline is simply to *know what you are teaching well enough to teach it.* The second guideline, even simpler to state but somewhat more likely to be neglected, is to *know who you are teaching.*

The first guideline, know what you are teaching well enough to teach it, seems so obvious that it hardly seems worth mentioning. However, it is worth noting that knowing what you are teaching and knowing what you are teaching well enough to teach it can be very different things. I learned this lesson the hard way during one of my earliest experiences as a teaching assistant. The instructor had covered a topic with the class, and she had asked me to review the topic, work through some examples, and answer questions during my weekly recitation section. The topic was one I was familiar with, and I foolishly saw no need for detailed preparation.

Although I teach computer science, my recitation section was held in a room that was equipped for chemistry demonstrations. A large, black, granite laboratory table with a built-in sink stood between the blackboard and the students. I confidently took my place between the laboratory table and the blackboard ready to begin. As I worked some sample problems, one of the students sat in the front row with the textbook open. Every few minutes he would raise

Teaching as a Balancing Act

his hand and, when called on, would point out a mistake I had made, or he would ask a question that, without fail, I was unable to answer. Now, there is certainly no shame in making a mistake while teaching a class, nor is there shame in having a student ask a question that cannot be answered; in fact this can be a very stimulating experience. However, in this instance, the truth was that I had made at least a dozen mistakes in as many minutes. And I was unable to answer my student's questions not because they were overly insightful but because I did not know the material well enough to be teaching it. In short, I was unprepared. I knew it, and the students knew it.

After about half an hour of stumbling, I grew increasingly frustrated with myself. At some point, in response to my frustration, I slammed my hand down on the laboratory table. (Did I mention the table was made of granite?) Fortunately, my hand missed the surface of the table. Unfortunately, it instead hit one of the metal spikes on the water faucet in the built-in sink. It hurt. A lot. I screamed, and cried a bit as well. Fortunately, nobody saw my tears because when my hand hit the faucet, it caused water to gush into the sink, where it ricocheted off some old books that had been discarded there, before hitting me in the face. There I stood, emotionally distressed by my lack of preparation, physically pained from my hand's collision with the faucet, soaking wet, and none too happy. Of course the class found the entire episode hilarious (clearly the high point of our meeting that day), and they burst into laughter every time I tried to resume discussion of the material. Needless to say, I never again showed up for class without knowing the material well enough to teach it.

Over time, I have come to see that it is only by knowing what I am teaching really well that I am able to make intelligent compromises between the conflicting objectives one inevitably encounters in teaching. Deciding, for example, when to use class time to reinforce the viewpoints of a textbook author and when to offer contradictory opinions to balance those views clearly requires deep, broad, and fresh knowledge of the material. Perhaps less obviously, knowing what you teach well enough to teach it does not just mean knowing the material well. It also means knowing how the material should be presented. Should general theories be presented first with specific examples to follow? What topics lend themselves best to a class discussion? How can ties be made between the current material and previous topics? Which topics can best be learned by having the students do a homework exercise? Of course, there are no simple answers to these questions, but the point is that making these decisions must be a thoughtful process that goes beyond merely understanding the content of the material being presented.

When deciding between pedagogical alternatives, I have found it extremely useful to have discussions with colleagues, both locally and at a distance. Many professional societies have special journals, conferences, and interest groups with a specific focus on pedagogy. For example, the major professional society for computer scientists has a group known as the Special Interest Group on Computer Science Education, which has been an invaluable source of information for me. Just as reading traditional research papers and attending research conferences can stimulate your own thinking about your discipline, reading papers and attending conferences about pedagogical issues in your discipline can stimulate your thinking about your teaching and can put you in a better position to balance competing objectives in your classroom.

Let's turn our attention to the second guideline mentioned earlier, know who you are teaching, by considering a scenario. Suppose you serve as an academic advisor for twenty students who are majoring in your discipline. Final semester grades have just been issued, and after reviewing grades for the students you advise, you are sending e-mail messages to congratulate some of them on particularly noteworthy performances and to express concern for others whose performances were substandard. One of the students is a junior who has earned a 3.2 on a 4.0 scale for the semester, and you note that a 3.2 is the minimum requirement for the dean's list at your school. Before reading on, take a moment to decide if you would send this student an e-mail and, if so, what, roughly, you would say.

Did you choose to send the e-mail? If so, did you congratulate the student on earning a 3.2? Or did you invite the student to visit your office to discuss what had gone wrong during the previous semester? Perhaps instead you challenged the student to work harder during the coming semester? Or did you do some combination of these things? Without the context that comes from knowing the student, there is no way to know the appropriate response. If, on the other hand, you know your students, it will be clearer how to respond. For example, if the student has never made the dean's list before and she has told you that making it is one of her goals, this will shape your response. If you also happen to know that the student achieved her goal while dealing with a midsemester case of mononucleosis, or the death of a grandparent, or an increase in the number of hours she had to work at an off-campus job, this will further shape your response. Undoubtedly, you would respond differently if you knew the student had previously earned straight A's, was very grade-conscious, and had previously shared with you that she was striving to graduate as the class valedictorian. Whatever the details, it is clear that knowing the student well can guide your response.

One might argue that the previous example has more to do with being an effective advisor than with being an effective teacher. In fact I believe that advising is a part of teaching and that one cannot be an effective teacher without

104

being an effective advisor as well, but it is also easy to offer examples to illustrate the benefits that knowing your students can bring to activities more specifically related to teaching. For example, each major in my department is required to complete a senior project of his or her choosing. Generally, students consult with faculty members as they decide on the project topic they wish to propose. Knowing that a particular student has a second major in mathematics, that another student is bilingual and interested in languages, that a third is trying to decide between attending graduate school and entering the workforce upon graduation, and that a fourth tends to lack confidence and has a history of being an underachiever can help me to advise these students as they each select a project topic that is appropriate.

To offer a slightly different example, I recall one semester when I had carefully constructed an assignment consisting of six homework problems. I told my students that they were to complete the assignment, which was due the following week, in pairs. Several days later a first-year student visited my office and announced, "I am stuck on problem four. I don't know how to do it at all." Since I did not yet know this student very well, rather than launching into a discussion about problem four, I decided to first spend a few moments getting to know the student and the context of his question. I asked a few questions, such as How is the course going in general? How long have you been working on problem four? How have you enjoyed working on a team for this assignment? How easy did you find problems one through three? I was particularly interested in the answer to the last question, because I knew that problem four was an extension of problem three. If the student had understood problem three, and could have explained it to me, I would have had a starting point for our discussion of problem four. However, to my surprise, the student responded to the last question by saying essentially: "I did not do problems one through three. I am working with Mary, and she is going to do the first three problems while I do the last three. Then we will meet and put our answers together to turn in."

After recovering from my initial shock, I realized that, in fact, I had never explained to the class how I wanted them to approach their teamwork (I wanted the students to work together on each problem), nor had I explained why I had asked them to work in teams or what I hoped this would accomplish. For that matter, I had not told them that the six problems were meant to be done in order or that the latter problems built on the earlier ones. Instead, I had mistakenly assumed all of this would be obvious. From taking a few minutes to get to know one of my students, not so much from a personal point of view, but from the point of view of trying to understand how he was approaching my course, I learned a lot that day. It became clear that the student and I did not need to talk about problem four (at least not at that point in time) but instead

Dave Berque

needed to talk about how he should approach the entire assignment. Thus what I learned helped me to resolve the tension between answering a student's question directly (how do I do problem four) and helping the student in a more indirect way. In the longer term, this experience also prompted me to adjust the amount of direction I give my classes when I assign team homework assignments.

I have the luxury of teaching at a small school with small classes. This affords many opportunities to interact with students informally, and it is even possible to invite all of the students I advise, or all the students enrolled in one of my classes, to join me for a meal. Even in situations where this is not possible (or desired) there are many other ways to get to know students, or at least some students. First, as illustrated above, when a student stops by during your office hours, try to talk about some contextual issues before delving into the problem at hand; these discussions are usually quite enjoyable, and I have often been surprised by the helpful information these discussions reveal. As another option, consider showing up for class five minutes early each day and chatting with students as they get settled. Use this time to learn the students' names and interests or to ask them what they thought of the assigned reading, how the homework is progressing, or how they feel about the pace of the course. You will almost certainly learn interesting and useful things, and you may even be able to make last-minute adjustments to your plans for the day to incorporate what you have learned.

Similarly, staying around the classroom for a few minutes after class ends gives you the chance to chat with a few of the students as they pack up. This is a particularly good time to ask whether class made sense that day. If so, you might ask them informally to summarize what they thought the main point was. If not, you might ask them what questions they have. These discussions will not only be helpful to the students you are talking to, but they may help you plan for your next class meeting as you try to decide how to compromise between launching forward with new material or reviewing the key points from the previous class first. The theme is a simple one: the more you know about your students, the better informed your resolution of competing objectives will be.

Asking students to provide written feedback on a regular basis is another, albeit slightly more formal, way to get to know students. For example, early in the semester you can ask the students to fill out a from on which they include basic biographical information, what they hope to get out of the course, a list of other related courses they have taken, etc. Later in the semester you might ask students to comment (with or without names attached) on anything they think you, the teacher, should know in order to improve the course, or you might ask more focused questions such as "What was the most important thing you learned today?" Some instructors even find it helpful to ask the same questions that will eventually appear on the end-of-semester evaluation form. Indeed, it does seem reasonable to try to obtain this information while you can still consider using it to adjust the current offering of the course.

Unfortunately, student comments on evaluation forms, while important, can be disheartening to read. I encountered such an example recently while teaching an upper-level course known as "Theory of Computation." As the name implies, this is a theoretical and abstract course that focuses more on the logical foundations of the discipline than on applications. There are two common ways to approach this course, and the instructor must embrace one or the other wholeheartedly or strike a compromise between the two. One approach is to motivate the course by building the case that a solid understanding of theoretical issues can assist students with their more applied interests. Thus applications of the theory are interjected at various points in the course. At the other extreme, an instructor can focus on the value of studying the material because of its inherent beauty. My own approach has tended to fall somewhere between the two extremes but, admittedly, with a significant bias toward the approach based on beauty.

On a recent set of evaluations for this course, one student wrote: "This course did not teach me anything that will help me with my future. However, it did help me to think more clearly." Apparently this student did not see the need for clear thinking in his or her future life! In some ways, I find this comment disheartening, while in other ways I find it encouraging (I think it is a good thing if one of my courses teaches a student to think more clearly, even if she or he does not immediately see the practical advantage of that). Without doubt, I am grateful for the comment, however, because it helped me to understand the perception of (at least one of) my students. And only by understanding their perceptions can I make intelligent decisions about future offerings of the course. In this case I need to reconsider the trade-off between presenting the study of theory as something that should be undertaken for the sake of its own beauty and explaining why the study of theory can enhance logical reasoning abilities, which in turn can indirectly help with all sorts of problems the students will encounter. I am not yet sure how I will resolve this tension, but armed with knowledge of the subject and an improved understanding of student perceptions, I am hopeful I will find a better compromise. Thus my journey continues, and so may it be for you.

Dave Berque

Teaching: What Has Worked for Me

Srinivasan "Rajan" Mahadevan

Is teaching the same as lecturing? I would define teaching as "edification" and lecturing as "oration." Teaching usually occurs through the medium of the lecture; I believe that it is important to recognize that one can be a great orator, but it does not automatically follow that one is a great educator.

There is also a difference between teaching a class and delivering a conference presentation. Conferees usually have a sophisticated understanding of the topic at hand. For that reason, they might be able to get the gist of the presentation even though the charts and slides are shown at the speed of time-lapse photographs. In contrast, the typical undergraduate student does not usually possess a basic knowledge of the subject at hand. One has to proceed through the topic at a pace that helps students build a knowledge base of the subject matter.

I believe that the goal of teaching is to train our students to become better thinkers. What can I tell them in class that they might find difficult to get on their own just by visiting the library?

I have taught thirteen different courses over many years, at several large state universities and at one community college in the United States. The class sizes have ranged from 30 to 220 students. I have also taught laboratory courses at two universities. The focus of my article is on undergraduate classes that are taught in the classroom. This does not address laboratory courses, fieldwork, seminars for groups of fewer than fifteen students, or other types of specialized courses. Rather, I am referring to the typical course that undergraduates take by attending classes in the classroom in order to meet a core course requirement.

A chapter on teaching methods or techniques must include the context in which these techniques and methods can be employed. A particular method might work well in one situation but not in some other. For example, in classes that involve physiology (e.g., the nervous system), either transparencies or PowerPoint slides are more useful than a blackboard. On the other hand, in situations that involve purely verbal comprehension, PowerPoint might not be as useful. Grading students for classroom participation might be more sensible in small classes than in large ones.

I am not criticizing teaching and assessment techniques. Rather, I am critical of the way in which these techniques have sometimes been used. For example, I am not against take-home examinations, term papers, or the use of transparencies and slides in the classroom. All of these can be useful if they are employed under the right set of circumstances. My criticism that various teaching and assessment techniques have been used in a faulty way is not in any way an indictment of the tools in and of themselves. To draw an analogy with baseball, a faulty pitching or batting performance is not necessarily the fault of either the ball or the bat. Further, a "typical" or "standard" method of assessing a batter's strong and weak points may not be a valid measure of that individual's batting ability.

The present essay is a distillation of my experiences as a teacher. This is an evaluation of what has worked for me. This chapter should therefore be viewed as the autobiography of a teacher.

The Syllabus

I have always viewed the syllabus as a contract between teacher and student. All of the information that the student needs to know about coursework should be included in the syllabus. It is important not simply to say how many tests, exams, or quizzes will be given during a semester. The exact number of questions that will be on each exam, test, or quiz and also all of the course policies should be spelled out. It is important to me that the students thoroughly understand all of my course policies. With that in mind, I give my students a quiz about the syllabus.

The Lecture

Classroom Lectures: Slides, Transparencies, or PowerPoint?

I used to believe that PowerPoint or at least slides were important for presenting lecture material in class. Not any longer. I am of the opinion that both PowerPoint and transparencies are distractions because students try to write down everything that is on each slide. This slows down the pace at which the material can be covered. Students copy the information blindly instead of paying attention to the lecture.

Nonetheless, our students do need to see the important point of a lecture, and not just hear it from us. For that reason I post a copy of my lecture plan on the Internet the day before a class so students can print out a copy and bring it with them to class.

Posting a copy of the lecture plan on the Internet has an added benefit over presenting the lecture material with PowerPoint. Students can see the entire layout of the lecture—throughout the lecture—without my having to slow down as I would have had to do using either PowerPoint or transparencies.

None of what I have said is intended to denigrate either PowerPoint or slides. For some topics, such as physiology and some areas of psychology (including behavioral neuroscience or sensation and perception), these tools can be immensely useful. Recently, when I was explaining a classic experiment to my students in an undergraduate cognitive psychology course, I used a PowerPoint slideshow to demonstrate the method used in that experiment. It was a lot easier to get students to understand and to appreciate the main point about the experiment that way compared to, say, trying to explain it only verbally or by using just the blackboard. In other words, PowerPoint and transparencies are often useful and sometimes virtually indispensable for relating the course material.

Focused Instruction

It is not fun to learn new things when there is a vast amount of information that has to be learned by students and assessed by teachers in a relatively short time. It is fun to learn new things if you do so at your own pace and if your understanding of the material is not being evaluated in any way. These two conditions seldom hold true when taking a class.

By "focused instruction" I mean that I like to be extremely specific about what I want my students to learn. For example, I do not simply say, "Read the first three chapters of your book." Many undergraduate students in large state universities simply cannot decide what is important and what is not. So I tell them exactly what they should read. For example, I say, "Begin reading at page 31, paragraph three, and read to page 34, paragraph five." I take full and complete responsibility when it comes to deciding exactly what I think is important for the student to know. I simply dislike passing the buck to the textbook.

Once I specify what I want students to study, I make sure that the questions for an exam come precisely from that material. Those students who attend classes regularly and study the class notes and the assigned material should not find any surprises in the exam.

Does this smack of "spoon-feeding"? The answer to this depends on how the course is taught and the nature of the reading material that is assigned to the students. The feedback that I get from students is that my exams are "medium"—neither too easy nor too hard. I do not believe I am spoon-feeding my students, because they must still think through and understand what they are reading.

Do You Have to Explain Something until Everyone in the Class Gets It?

The amount of explanation needed depends on the size of the class. In a small class, it might be possible to explain something until everyone gets it. I tend to monitor the reactions of my students and get a feel for whether they are getting the information. If I feel that they are not comprehending, then I stop and ask if they have any questions. The responsibility of the student is to make sure that he or she understands the material and, if not, to ask questions.

Common Sense

I have heard teachers say about some topic, "Statistics is common sense." Really? And, if so, to whom? I hold the view that it is a fashion (I hope it is only a fad) for people to say that some particular subject matter is common sense. The truth of the matter is that any subject can be seen as routine logic—for people who have a background and a knowledge base in that particular subject. In other words, to a physicist, rocket science might be straightforward, and to a statistician, statistics might be intuitive. For those of us who teach classes the subject matter might be easy. But though it may be reasonable and fundamental to *us,* that does not mean that the subject has to be common sense to our students.

Methods of Assessment

Ideally an essay exam should be the mode of assessment in those classes where the students' critical thinking and analytical skills are challenged, as it gives them an opportunity to demonstrate their level of understanding of a topic in their own words. This method might work with upper-division courses in which there are a small number of students. It may not be practical to give essay exams to classes of over fifty students—unless one has a T.A.

I have used the following version of an essay exam in some of my classes in which the number of students have been fewer than forty. I say that each answer "must be written in fifty words or less and in grammatically correct sentences." There is nothing sacrosanct about an upper limit of fifty words—one could make it a hundred words instead. The idea, though, is to force students to think clearly about what they wish to say instead of rambling on and on in the hope that the correct answer will be contained in the rambling.

As an alternative to the essay exam, the multiple-choice exam has the distinct advantage that a large number of exams can be graded rapidly. In theory, a multiple-choice exam can surely also be constructed in a way that tests students' critical thinking skills. Nonetheless, in most undergraduate classes the multiple-choice exam is primarily used as a method of testing whether the student has understood basic facts.

I dislike having my students in large classes write term papers. The goal of asking students to write term papers is to encourage them to think critically about some topic and then to express their thoughts in a scholarly manner that also permits creativity of expression. I will argue that none of these conditions can be attained in a typical undergraduate class. For one thing, grading term papers is an extremely labor-intensive process—especially with classes over thirty or forty students. Then there is the problem that students (in my experience) rarely care to read the feedback we give them on their papers. Finally, term papers make sense only if a given student is required to submit several drafts of a paper—so that the professor can give feedback on each draft and the student can then see how performance improved across drafts. Term papers are ideal for very small classes (say, around fifteen students) or for students participating in supervised research, such as working with a professor on a laboratory project.

I am against giving points for classroom participation. This method of assessment might work in small classes of around ten students where the instructor and students all interact extensively on a one-to-one basis. Barring this sort of situation, I think we should not give points for classroom participation because it is impossible to measure it empirically. There are "talkers" (garrulous individuals who say a lot simply for the sake of saying something) and then there are "sleepers" (soporific-looking individuals who are fine students but who do not say a word in class—possibly because they are shy). Personality factors can influence who speaks up and who does not, and therefore, classroom participation may not be a valid method of assessing the degree of learning.

What about group projects with, say, three to five students working on a project together? I have mixed feelings about such projects. What I have heard from colleagues and from students is that not everyone pulls his or her weight equally on such projects. That seems to be the typical response. The one time I did use this method, it worked well—with an honors-level psychology course in which the students were very motivated.

When showing students a video, I make sure that I give them a handout on the video. Again, the purpose of the handout is to make sure that students know what information they are supposed to extract from the video.

In sum, I would like to say that any method of assessment can be made to work, as long as the tasks that are assigned to students are very carefully related to both learning and assessment goals.

Validity of Assessment

The validity of assessment, I believe, depends upon our keeping examinations extremely focused so that we test our students on what they are supposed to know.

At the very minimum, I believe grades tell us whether our students are well prepared for the exams we give. The much larger question of whether grades represent genuine learning is not something for us to decide. We can help students only by giving them a foundation in some topic. They may or may not enjoy the course content at all. It is not our job to try to get students hooked on the subject matter. It is a fact that most students take our classes not because they want to, but because they have to. If some of our students are inspired to learn more about the subject, and if they attribute their inspiration to us, I think we have accomplished enough.

What Do You Do When Things Go Wrong?

The Missed Exam

One semester, I overslept and failed to show up for a midterm exam. I had to devise a new grading scale that all of my students found entirely satisfactory and just. I will not go into detail about the changes I made in the grading scale; nonetheless, I learned a lesson from this incident: to make sure that I leave copies of my exams in a place where my T.A. can access them.

Four Questions from the Review Day

In a course that I am currently teaching, I conducted a review session during the class before an exam. During the course of that review, I inadvertently covered some new material—over and above what I was supposed to have been reviewing. I asked four questions from that extra material. After the exam, one student pointed out to me that he did not attend the review session because he did not know that extra material would be covered. He said that if he had known this, he would have attended the review session. And so he suggested that the four questions from the new material were not fair.

What did I do? I simply discarded those four questions and gave all of my students credit for them. I believe that was the fairest way to deal with the matter.

What If the Classroom Is Locked?

In one class that I taught (the same one for which I had overslept for an exam!) the final was on a Saturday morning, and the classroom door was locked. I did not have to call the police because another faculty member in that building had a key to that classroom, and he opened the door for me. It is worth pointing out that the police do not have the key to open every door on campus (I got this information from a police officer). And so what would I have done in the worst-case scenario—that the students could not take the exam? I leave that one to you to decide!

The Cell Phone

I usually get the cell phone numbers of a few students from every class that I teach. If some emergency arises, then I can call one of those students and get through to the class.

Concluding Remarks

Good teaching requires that one acquire a number of skills, one of which is being a good lecturer. Effective teaching does not require that we make any attempt to get every one of our students hooked on the subject matter. We are teachers and not talk show hosts. Good teaching does not require that we try to entertain our students for much of time.

If one assumes that the thing of greatest intrinsic interest to human beings is to maximize happiness, or at least to try to minimize pain, then this is what the world's most profound and enlightened religious teachers have attempted and failed (or at least have not completely succeeded in doing). One could therefore ask why we should or could ever hope to inspire a hundred or so undergraduate students about topics that are of little interest to them.

The world operates on tension and apprehension. A vast majority of our students have very little intrinsic interest in the courses that they take. The examination system, pressure of grades, and escalating cost of education all combine to make university education an aversive experience. Our job as teachers is to try to minimize this aversion to the extent possible by having clear-cut course objectives, focused instruction, and a fair and reasonable method for assessment and evaluation.

Srinivasan "Rajan" Mahadevan

A Letter from James Buchanan

James Buchanan

Perhaps, in my own case, I have tended to underplay the importance of having been forced to go through the boring courses in education at Middle Tennessee State Teacher College, including practice teaching, which may have really helped me in teaching. In addition, I know that my mother's insistence, against my will, that I take a private course in public speaking helped me both in classroom performance and in all other formal and informal speaking.

As for more specific "secrets" of success in teaching, let me mention only a few, which may or may not be generally relevant. I have personally never had the slightest problem with discipline, in any form. Why? I think it stems from my own personality, which tends toward the authoritarian, but which does command respect from students. Personality cannot, of course, be laid on deliberately, but an important element is self-confidence, which can, to a degree, be generated by investment in preparation. Early on in my teaching, I learned that it is useful always to have available a set of notes upon which the teaching proceeds. This set of notes provides a backup for possible lapses in flow of discussion. Relatedly, I have always, even now, prepared a new set of notes for each course, even if I have taught the same course many times.

During the last twenty years or so of my active teaching career, I taught second-year graduate students for the most part. I found it very productive to require a lot of written work, think pieces rather than research papers, for the most part short papers on assigned topics, graded not only on analytical content but on style, grammar, etc.

Students in prior years who have become successful have evaluated my teaching by suggesting that the best element in it was the sense that I was working out with them my own ideas that were going into my research at the time. They sensed that they were a central part of the whole exercise of working out ideas that were advancing beyond the received conventional wisdom in the subject matter at hand. And several of these former students, who have become quite successful, attribute a part of their own success to this initial exposure to ongoing research effort, which is itself, a means of producing self-confidence.

It's Wednesday: Take Two

Louis J. Gross

An enticing property of teaching regularly is the rejuvenating power of knowing that another "take" is just a day or two away. There is elation—at least for perfectionists—associated with the reflection "Well, I didn't really get that concept across today, so let's try another tact on Wednesday."

Such simple dreams are rarely fulfilled. Pragmatically, the syllabus-drive to get through what we, or some curriculum committee or accreditation board, have deemed an appropriate body of material works against revisiting our failures, real or imagined. This is when true leadership comes into play, when we pull the class along to clarify a concept, perhaps even admit failure while pointing out the importance of their comprehension. Rerouting to success can include linking the concept to something new that may illumine the foundation the students did not grasp previously, thus assuaging the need to "cover new material" while increasing the fraction who understand the central concept.

Developing a metaphor that places a concept in an alternative perspective can be useful for the teacher in other ways. A central theme of the calculus reform movement that swept through United States mathematics departments in the early 1990s is that modes of learning vary from student to student. Enlisting multiple metaphors (in calculus, this means algebraic, graphical, and numerical) to address the same concept increases the fraction of the class who "get it." The bane of college mathematics education in the United States is that the curriculum is developed by, and the courses are taught by, those who didn't have much difficulty "getting it" in the first place. Forcing ourselves to consider alternative routes to student comprehension empowers us to review our assumptions and perhaps discover why it came so naturally to us in the first place. This should increase the likelihood that we assist students in developing intuition about the field rather than merely enhancing their skills.

Undergraduate mathematics texts are full of alternative examples designed to elicit comprehension by providing contexts that students can supposedly relate to. It is tempting to offer numerous examples for any single concept. For example, by associating the idea of a derivative in calculus with multiple instances of instantaneous rates of change—individual weight change, interest income in a bank account, population growth rates, the speed of a car, chemical reaction rates, etc.—we hope that at least one of these resonates with each student. This plethora can distract from the main point, though, and confuse conscientious students who may feel obliged to follow the intent of each example. Ideal examples resonate with the vast majority of students' life experiences. These are not limited to drugs, sex, and rock and roll, although those may be good places to start. All students have had experience with drugs—at least over-the-counter medications—and have an inherent interest in how they affect them. This provides an excellent basis for mathematics, chemistry, and biology courses, since it allows the professor to draw upon students' personal experiences as well as their natural interests.

One possible means to develop student intuition is to employ a case-study approach throughout a course or section of a course. Mathematical modeling courses often work this way, taking multiple views of the same underlying problem to illustrate how different approaches lead to new insights. Different sections of a course might introduce new topics that enhance the students' skills; their intuition about some underlying problem expands as alternative viewpoints are developed.

In my entry-level math courses for life science students, I use the problem of projecting future land-use (e.g., loss of agricultural lands to housing developments) to illustrate the application of different quantitative methods. Aerial photographs or satellite images over time provide students with easily interpreted changes across a landscape. News articles on topics such as urban sprawl or the effects of fire-control (which allows the buildup of large amounts of combustible material) prompt numerous questions that students themselves develop from the images. In discussion, students quickly ascertain that in order to infer the impact of actions such as zoning laws or firefighting, something beyond simply analyzing images is needed. This provides an entrée to the use of mathematical objects called matrices, which summarize the situation without taking into account all of the spatial complexities inherent in the images. From this point on in the course, new concepts associated with matrix algebra are related to the intuition developed about landscapes from the images and from computer-based simulations that mimic landscape change over time.

Another advantage of a case study that permeates a course or section of a course is that it can foster interdisciplinary perspectives. Landscape change touches topics in biology (vegetative succession changes following fire), sociology, urban planning, demography, and geography. Similarly, student comprehension of biological evolution can be enhanced by using it as an example of optimization in calculus courses, assuming evolution arises as a central theme and not just another add-on example. Typical optimization examples in calculus courses involve finding the largest area that can be enclosed with a certain amount of fencing or the maximum volume of a box given a certain area of cardboard. These are not nearly as interesting as analyzing the cardiovascular branching system in mammals to determine whether observed branching patterns are in any sense optimal for maximizing blood flow throughout a particular region. Given the great antipathy among the general populace concerning evolution, exposure to the conceptual foundation outside a formal biology course could increase student appreciation of the fundamental importance of the ideas of natural selection throughout the life sciences.

Essential to critical thinking and problem solving is the process of deciding what to include—this is why I have called modeling the process of "selective ignorance." Success in critical thinking involves deciding what is extraneous to a situation and what is essential. Student abhorrence of "word problems" in math courses derives in part from the requirement that they select the key variables and the relationships between them while ignoring all else. The art of doing this effectively depends not just on experience but on intuition. This intuition is not something we construct from the ground up in our classroom. Students come to us with prior intuition that we must either enhance or refute. Indeed, refuting misconceptions may be the most important teaching we do. This is especially the case if we can assist students in coming to correct conclusions themselves rather than merely handing down our beliefs to them.

From a curricular perspective, the notion of "multiple takes" is particularly applicable to undergraduate education. Despite the oft-stated arguments for interdisciplinarity, we do not often link concepts between courses in different fields. It is a rare student who can readily internalize a concept after one exposure. Repetition at the curricular level has advantages that cannot be obtained by exposing students to a concept multiple times in a single course. The success of writing-across-the-curriculum programs is one indication that skills are enhanced by application in a variety of learning contexts. This indicates to students that ideas are not isolated to one field but are important in many. It offers students multiple viewpoints to build upon what they already know and provides them multiple chances to "get it." Therefore the onus is on educators, if we deem a concept to be critical to success for students in our field, to work with colleagues outside the field to ensure that the concept is incorporated in other courses our students take. Happily, funding agencies such as the National Science Foundation recognize this and offer a variety of programs to encourage interdisciplinary collaborations that advance undergraduate education.

Louis J. Gross

The Hornet's Opinion

Dorothy Wallace

> When we are young we generally estimate an opinion
> by the size of the person that holds it, but later we find
> that is an uncertain rule, for we realize that there are
> times when a hornet's opinion disturbs us more than
> an emperor's.
>
> —Mark Twain, "An Undelivered Speech,"
> March 25, 1895

I seem to remember getting my first job tutoring math when I was thirteen, so I suppose I should be celebrating thirty years of teaching math just about now. I love the way mathematics reaches from the very abstract down to the terribly applied particular, and all the ways of using it to look at the world. Doing mathematics is such a joy, yet it is the joy that is so hard to communicate in the classroom. I think my most effective teaching has probably been one-to-one, supervising various honors theses and internships, watching a single student grow over the course of a year or more into a budding mathematician with a unique individual taste for the subject. The classroom situation is a much greater challenge.

Most students come into the classroom already interested in many things other than mathematics. For the last five years I have been the principal investigator for a large project, Math across the Curriculum, which, taking this observation as its premise, has introduced over two dozen courses integrating mathematics with other subjects and has influenced many others. I have been involved personally with a half dozen of these—math and art, various math and literature courses, math and physics, math and biology. In addition to the expected activities in a math class—lectures, problem solving, computer exercises, group work—suddenly there are art critiques, laboratory experiments, data sets, discussions of literature, extensive writing. Allowing the whole world into the math classroom puts the teacher in the position of the ultimate non-expert. Now we really are a learning community.

As a member of the community born in my own classroom, I learned a lot about how to teach. I learned that the way art teachers respond publicly to homework is a great model for approaching the various answers students give to truly open-ended math problems. I learned that the process of rewriting papers is really a fractal, and that if you explain it that way you will get better work from your students. I discovered that reading Copernicus gives college-age students a new respect for the geometry they learned in high school—a respect for geometry as a deep intellectual advance rather than for its utility. I found out that "group theory," a branch of mathematics rarely explored by students in other majors, makes sense to art students if presented in the context of textile design. I realized that "useful" really is in the eye of the beholder, and a classroom contains many different beholders.

This essay offers the opportunity to consolidate a lot of observations, experiments, and errors into a few potentially helpful principles. Of course, many of these have been stated before, sometimes in other contexts. I will wait until the end to offer sources. I also plan to spare the reader detailed accounts of the gross errors I have made along the way, although these might be the more entertaining stories. I will try to stick to my own observations while casually acknowledging the fact that they are not in the least original.

The Teacher Is the Least Important Person in the Classroom

The instructor is only one person in a room of, say, thirty people. The other twenty-nine are struggling to learn new material, despite coming in with a mixed bag of interests and background. These twenty-nine are the ones who will learn something during the semester. They will struggle trying to read the text (especially if it is mathematics). They will put hours into the homework. They will be upset with themselves when they get stuck. They will take tests, an activity nobody likes. They will get grades, and some won't like their grades. They will get sick or have personal crises that interfere with their ability to get work done, but they will get most of it done anyway.

One of the thirty has a different job. Simply put, the teacher's job is to make it as easy as possible for the students to learn as deeply as possible. In the end, it will not matter whether her lecture was clear or muddy, whether she possessed a clever turn of phrase or told an amusing joke. All that will matter is whether the students learned new things and remembered them long enough afterward to use them. The teacher functions as signpost, traffic cop, Pied Piper, Zen master, or collie dog, all in the effort to move students in a particular direction. But the journey belongs to the pupil.

You Probably Don't Know What They Are Thinking

Let me say this more strongly. You *don't* know what they are thinking. The students look happy and intelligent, but they actually didn't understand anything you just said. They look confused, but actually they just realized what you really meant. One asks a question that leads you to believe he misunderstood a definition you just introduced, when in reality he misunderstood a concept last week and only now is it coming to light. You really don't know where they are unless you ask them, over and over in a variety of ways.

As any composition teacher will tell you, clarity of thought leads to clarity of expression, not the other way around. Writing, therefore, is a particularly good way to discover whether students have made sense out of the main ideas of the course. Fragmented, unorganized knowledge can't be retrieved later when it is needed for new applications. The narrative structure lacking in most mathematics texts and courses seriously impedes the ability of the student to retain information. On the other hand, that lack of structure can be an asset if students are asked explicitly to provide the narrative themselves, assuming that the material is coherent enough to make such an activity possible.

Confusion Is the First Step in Learning

This is more than a statement about the emotional responses of students. The deepest form of learning happens when we challenge our entire manner of approaching a concept in order to form a new schema. This kind of learning must happen in almost every mathematics class in order for a student to advance through difficult and abstract material. It is an extremely confusing process, requiring a fairly long time frame to resolve.

For readers who do not enjoy the beauty of mathematics every day, I will offer an example that should be familiar from your high school education in algebra. Here is a simple education with one variable, x. Just imagine it. This letter, x, is a number that we do not yet know, and the equation is a little puzzle we must solve to identify x. Oh, yes, there are rules we have to follow to solve it, but we could also keep guessing until we found an x that works. Standardized tests can't tell these behaviors apart.

Now here is another equation with both an x and a y in it. What are we supposed to do with it? Our x is no longer a particular number that we have to find—it will vary depending on what y is. So the equation as a whole is no longer a little puzzle to solve. Instead, it expresses a relationship between the two quantities x and y, and the question "what is x?" doesn't even make sense any more. Now we are befuddled. We aren't sure what this equation is trying to tell us. We don't know what sort of questions it can answer for us. We have to learn to think about x in a whole new way.

Worse yet, here are the "quadratic equations in x and y." These are a whole class of equations, each of which expresses a relationship of a particular kind. What can we say about this collection of equations as a whole? What common properties do they share? Why have people grouped them together to study?

Once again, we are confused. To make sense of this inquiry we need to think of each equation as an object with certain properties so that we can classify them and make general statements. But how can we think of equations as objects? On what basis should we divide them into classes for study? It is very confusing. It should be confusing at first, because the confusion is a sign that we understand we are in a new and very different situation. Acknowledging appropriate confusion aloud is a helpful and reassuring gesture to the student.

Good mathematics students have achieved the emotional fortitude to deal with their own confusion without getting frustrated and angry, a skill we rarely bother to teach explicitly. Those who go on to do research in mathematics have actually learned to enjoy the sensation of being puzzled by a problem. A course in which the student is never confused is a course in which no deep learning takes place. Acquisition of facts is the lowest form of learning and can be achieved easily by any literate individual with access to a library.

Read the Literature

As I mentioned near the beginning of this essay, none of these tips are the least bit original. The first bit of advice is inspired by the life work of Paulo Freire, the famous Brazilian educator who wrote *Pedagogy of the Oppressed*. It is also explored beautifully in bell hook's book *Teaching to Transgress*. The second piece of advice can be found everywhere in educational literature, yet still comes as a surprise. You could say it is part of the legacy of Piaget, who attempted to find out what students really were thinking. My own favorite reference is *The Having of Wonderful Ideas* by Eleanor Duckworth, which gives a beautiful account not only of what is in the student's mind but also how to make the best use of it. The phrase "Confusion is the first step in learning" is attributable to my high school geometry teacher, James Herbinaux of Redwood City, California, although the supporting description of cognitive stages in algebra can be found in Eon Harper, "Ghosts of Diophantus."[1] To those versed in educational literature this last reference may seem less important than the previous two, but to a mathematics teacher it is of equal value. Mathematics teaching, more than any other kind, depends on making constructive use of confusion.

So I will close by inviting the reader of this essay, whose field of expertise and range of interests I cannot begin to predict, to become acquainted with some of my own favorite authors. If you have a short attention span for professional educational jargon and a strong desire to flee from tedious accounts of educational studies, you could not do better that to read these authors. Their wisdom, humor, and strong opinions are excellent companionship for the road ahead.

126

Note

1. Eon Harper, "Ghosts of Diophantus," *Educational Studies in Mathematics* 18 (1987): 75–90.

Part Three

III. Contexts: Teaching and Culture

Creating a Sense of Community in the Classroom

Orville Vernon Burton

My students' attitudes about race have changed over the years. When I first moved to Illinois, we were still in the aftermath of the Civil Rights Movement. My students seemed to believe that the United States was tilted so that all the evils rolled down into the South. As I taught race relations over the years, this view has shifted. I still remember in the 1980s when I was teaching a course on race relations and a white student came up to me and said, "Professor Burton, you don't understand; you are from the South, where all races of people are cordial." She went on to explain in terminology very similar to the old proslavery "bestiality" arguments that "'those people' in South Side Chicago are like animals." The South has now become in popular movies and books a place where race relations are OK. Now it is the inner-city North that has the problem. African American as well as white students reflect this naïve view.

Perhaps an even more important way that the teaching of race relations has changed is in its reflection and awareness of the diversity of America. The increasing Hispanic and Asian American population and the recognition of Native American rights (especially with the University of Illinois' retention of the "Chief" as its athletic symbol, clearly an insult to Native Americans) have come to be more important in the teaching of race relations. When I began teaching race relations in 1974, one of the questions we explored was which came first, race or slavery. Of course, this would not have been a question of significance if it did not have ideological implications relevant to our own times and the Civil Rights Movement. If the institution of slavery grew very slowly and was not complete until the beginning of the eighteenth century, then racial prejudice was not the inherent and automatic reaction of the British and European people when meeting Africans for the first time. The corollary of this line of thinking is that the eradication of racial prejudice would come with the elevation of economic status of the subjugated group, and prejudice would melt away quickly. It's a relatively happy view.

On the other hand, if the reaction of the English and Europeans when first meeting Africans was to enslave them, then racial prejudice may be so ingrained in human nature that the truly integrated society we want is impossible. This sort of dichotomous thinking worked well for students to wrestle with in those years. But as we become more aware of the many sides and forms of racism in our multiethnic society, this dichotomy does not ring true. Now we talk about the creation of race and the creation of "whiteness." The relationship of class and gender to race relations has to occupy a large portion of any class. I like to present these arguments to students as scholars developed and changed the arguments over the years. Then I have the students ponder why historians wrestling with these issues might have come up with the theories they did at a particular time.

The issues of affirmative action and minority rights, especially the end of segregation under the 1964 Civil Rights Act and the emergence of voting rights under the 1965 Voting Rights Act, have also influenced the circumstances in which I teach about race. I do not hesitate to bring in my courtroom experiences as an expert witness for minority plaintiffs in voting rights or discrimination cases. Students learn, just as I learned, that the discrimination against Latinos in El Centro, California, was very much like the discrimination against African American laborers in the South. I often share with them how people in El Centro elected African Americans to the school board, although African Americans were only about 3 percent of the population, but would not elect Hispanics, who were over 40 percent. These sorts of real-life examples help students understand the relevance of history in race relations and how important it is that all peoples have their stories told. A recent case where a San Diego African American postal worker was called "boy" by white coworkers really engaged the interest of my class. They tried to understand why that term is demeaning to an African American male and does not have the same negative connotation for whites. This was precisely the issue that I was asked to explain to the court. Thus, seeing how history is used in the courtroom helped my students understand the power of history.

I regularly teach both halves of the U.S. history survey, and have since 1971. At the University of Illinois, I lecture with as many as 750 students in an auditorium. Students attend lectures twice a week and meet with a graduate teaching assistant in discussion sections once a week. Early in my career, I would try to lead one discussion section of the survey, and that helped me do better as a lecturer. But finally the realities of tenure and pressures of time convinced me to give up the additional courses.

I do not like the large surveys. Any good teaching done in those courses is done by graduate teaching assistants in the discussion sections. Given that this is what the students have to take, I am always trying to find effective teaching techniques. One approach I try in these large surveys is to be deliberately outrageous on a controversial issue. I establish with the teaching assistants ahead of time how they will handle the issue in discussion section. The teaching assis-

Creating a Sense of Community in the Classroom

tants and I take opposing viewpoints, forcing the students to challenge at least one of the "authority" figures in the class. That seems to work very well. By the way, supervising up to nine graduate teaching assistants and helping them with their teaching is also part of teaching the survey.

My first year at the University of Illinois when I was teaching the survey, I was called in by our most distinguished U.S. historian. I am sure he meant well, but he informed me that there were many problems with my teaching: my clothing (wearing dungarees to teach in), my southern accent, my assignment of social history books like Robert Gross's *The Minutemen and Their World,* and my determination to discuss "social class." But he thought my biggest problem was that I was confusing students by discussing how different historians thought differently about issues. "This is the only history course that most of these students will ever take," he told me, "and they need to know the *facts.*" I disagreed. If this was the only history course students would ever take, it was all the more important that they know that historians disagree over what the *facts* are as well as over interpretations. I still believe that.

I want students to be able to use critical, analytical skills and learn to think, not just memorize facts. Students do need information, but it is much more important for them to understand that someone puts that information together and that biases and prejudices always affect how we put order into the wonderfully complex chaos of history. I personally hope for learning miracles—that my teaching might inspire students to confront their passivity, to think about and apply social justice issues at the grassroots level.

I think that we all think we try to cover too many facts. That is why I originally wrote some computer-drill and map exercises: so that students could master the "facts" and then we might hope to discuss the important issues of history. I am careful to explain that there is too much to cover and that we are leaving things out, but whether the source is a lecture or the textbook, nothing is ever left out by default, and students should always question and challenge me and the textbook.

Ultimately, trying to do too much in terms of both coverage and depth led me to develop an overall teaching philosophy—a mission statement and goals for each class. Over the years, I have modified both mission statements and goals, and in the last few years I got great advice from the University of Illinois Instructional Resources Office. They helped me rewrite my goals for each class from the perspective of the students rather than from my perspective.

In the basic American history surveys, I try to help students attain a solid grasp of the narrative sweep of the period covered by the course: periodization, principal events, ideas, people, and trends and why they are significant. I also try

133

to give them critical reasoning tools through written assignments and class discussion. Here, it is especially important to introduce the idea of differing viewpoints and interpretations. Finally, and most important, I encourage students to construct and present arguments of their own, always having the students incorporate both primary and secondary sources. These projects are essential if we want to give students a sense of the complexity inherent in society. In other words, while I acknowledge that students do need some of the traditional coverage of the survey, I think that, within the context of the survey, a teacher can design research projects that allow students to develop a deeper understanding. Then they may learn how to apply those skills to other problems. We are trying to get students to think critically.

I also stress in the early lectures that all historians, including myself and the authors of the textbooks, select certain facts, and how someone selected these facts tells us something. I try to get students to ask why we are stressing a particular set of facts and to ask themselves if other groups (Native Americans, Hispanics, African Americans, Asian Americans, non-Europeans) would have used the same facts or interpreted them the same ways. In other words, I challenge students to imagine different voices telling the story. Excellent examples for this are in the works of sociologist James W. Loewen, who wrote two thought-provoking books, *Lies My Teacher Told Me: Everything Your American History Textbook Got Wrong* and *Lies across America: What Our Historic Sites Get Wrong.* Since Loewen studied high school history books in the first of these works, and since so many of our students in the survey are just one year removed from high school, I find the book and its examples work very well. Thus I might begin with the myth that Loewen uses of the Dutch purchase of New York for twenty-four dollars' worth of beads and then take the class through an analysis of the event.

I supplement my survey courses with assignments that involve the former-slave narratives collected by the WPA (now conveniently available on the Web). First, I have students read selected essays on the problems of working with these narratives. I have one exercise comparing how two African Americans relate stories of their ancestors who were involved in two slave revolts, the Stono and the Denmark Vessey rebellions. It is interesting to note that most students miss the fact that both people being interviewed were born after slavery. That leads to the question of why the white interviewer was so interested in these stories. Also, both of these African Americans are proud of their ancestors, and students see how that contradicts the essays' warning to readers that the narrators tend to give "conservative" answers to please white interviewers.

Another exercise with the former-slave narratives uses the example of former slave Susan Hamlin, interviewed twice, once by a white interviewer and once by an African American interviewer. These two narratives are available and analyzed in Mark Lytle and James Davidson's *After the Fact: The Art of Historical Detection*. However, I want students to do the analyzing. I typed up the originals and distributed them to students, leaving out identifying pieces of information. Few students figure out that it is the same interviewee in both interviews. In the huge survey course, I break the students down into small groups to do this exercise. It works very well as they go through the process of discovering that the same person is being interviewed but telling two different stories.

I've had my share of worst teaching moments, too. One time a planned lesson went awry because a student tried to "rescue" me. Until it became rather notorious and students expected it and visitors came to the first class just to see it, I used to have two other faculty or two graduate students come into class and attack me verbally and start a mock fight. They would then rush out of the room, or someone would come in and drag them out. Then I asked the students' "help." I asked them to write up what had happened, describing the incident and the people. It was an excellent way to introduce students to "first-hand" records because their accounts differed radically. One time, unfortunately, one of the students came to my defense, and I had to grab him to keep him from harming the professor who was pretending to attack me.

Another time I had an experience during an exercise where I ask students about stereotypes: What do they think about when they hear the word "southerner"? "Yankee"? "midwesterner"? I was on the platform in front of about 750 students at the time, and a friend of mine, Franky Davis, from Ninety Six, South Carolina, my hometown, was visiting. Franky is one of those "hell-of-a-fellow" sorts described by W. J. Cash in *Mind of the South*. Franky would follow me everywhere, wearing his construction outfit, his steel-toed boots, and a knife at his side. As I was doing this exercise and the students were responding to the stereotype of the "southerner," some suggested terms like *racist* and *ignorant*. Franky lost his temper and started to go after the student. I had to jump after Franky to get him out of the class. That was a bad situation, but another student broke the ice when she piped up, "How about *violent?*"

I like teaching history because history underpins a liberal arts education. As an art, history encourages intellect and spirit. As a discipline, history sharpens analytical rigor. American history should be inclusive, meaningful, and relevant to every age; it is inescapable and every person plays a part. When we learn to make judgments about historical interpretations, we are also learning to make judgments about the daily news, conventional wisdom, and even our own ideas. I am firm in my belief that teaching a critical perspective is essential, not for history alone, but for all aspects of modern life.

135

Diversity-Conscious Teaching: From the Beanbag to the Bottom Line

Richard D. Bucher

As a teacher at Baltimore City Community College (BCCC), I have spent the last twenty-eight years educating others and myself about diversity and the increasingly prominent role it plays in our lives. To this end, I have created and engaged in a variety of activities and initiatives that involve my students, colleagues, and the larger community. Broadening my thinking and expanding my knowledge base in the area of diversity have enabled me to relate more effectively to my students, many of whom share cultures and histories that are far different from mine. Nurturing the connection between my students and me has been an extremely difficult process. It is a process that is intellectual as well as affective, uneven, and at times uncomfortable.

Perhaps the best way to describe the process of infusing diversity into what and how I teach is to examine the evolution of relationships in my sociology classes. Research conducted by the author[1] and published by the American Association of Higher Education points to the critical importance of diversity as it relates to interrelationships among students, the subject matter, and the instructor. By engaging diversity over the course of a semester, my students and I learn more about each other and sociology. The result is greater student achievement.

Any discussion of my teaching has to start with my students. BCCC is an urban community college, with a population that is approximately 88 percent African American and 73 percent female. Many BCCC students are economically disadvantaged, work multiple jobs, support their families, and raise their children with little or no help. Recently, I read a newspaper article in which a student compared her isolated existence at a nearby four-year college to living in a bubble. My students do not have that luxury.

I am privileged to teach students who bring a vast array of life experiences to the classroom. However, their potent stories of struggle and sacrifice, achievement and failure, and pain and joy typically remain hidden. The key is to tap this diversity and learn from it. However, the cultural baggage that students bring into class can make this difficult. It does not take much to push students out the door. Many have been ignored, stereotyped, and stigmatized. Many have low expectations of themselves. Often, they have been taught to settle for mediocrity. For some, just getting to class on a given day is a monumental achievement, while for others, getting a degree means avoiding the violence that has taken the lives of friends and family members.

My own diversity is something I share openly with my classes. On the first day of class, I spend time talking about my family, my twenty-seven-year-old autistic son, my education at Howard University—a historically black institution, and other sensitizing experiences that continue to transform my thinking about diversity. Later on, I take students back to my childhood—growing up in an all-white, suburban, and ethnically homogenous community that is totally foreign to many of them. I recall times when I found it difficult to look beyond a person's disability, even though my son has a disability. By sharing who I am with my students in a very open, intimate way, I begin to shape the classroom climate and let my students know something about my hidden diversity and "where I'm coming from." We come to realize that, in many ways, we share the same fears and hang-ups when we interact with people who may not look, talk, or act like us. My sharing also sets the stage for a semester-long process that requires a tremendous amount of understanding, empathy, sharing, and cognitive development on both of our parts.

Engaging diversity requires us to examine ourselves and our worlds. Values become clearer and change is possible when students acknowledge their own diversity and all of its manifestations. In one class exercise, I ask students: "Imagine that you are being forced to change your gender or your race/ethnicity or your sexual orientation. Which would you change and why?" Uncovering layers of power and privilege and coming to grips with how we feel about changing our minority and majority statuses make this a powerful lesson. But its effect is minimal unless self-exploration leads to understanding and in turn serves as the foundation for the development of flexible thinking and other competencies. While the cumulative effect of this kind of self-exploration can be profound, it requires time and persistence.

Infusing diversity into the curriculum is not always planned. It may occur simply because the instructor actively listens to the multiple perspectives found in a typical community college classroom. For example, in one of my sociology classes, I asked for feedback on the first reading assignment. One of my students took issue with the tone of the first chapter and, in particular, an anecdote about the "wilding" incident in New York City's Central Park, in which a number of black men assaulted a female jogger. While the author of the book used this example to illustrate the sociological perspective, the student commented that this was just another example of how black men are portrayed as violent and criminal. Other students quickly sided with her, and an intense, heated discussion followed. I suggested that they write the author and express their views. They did, and the author responded immediately. He expressed an interest in visiting our college and talking with the students face to face. Shortly thereafter, he traveled a considerable distance to meet them and discuss their concerns. This dialogue helped him understand that the tone of the first chapter caused many of my students to shut down and stop learning. He then agreed to eliminate this example from the next edition, and he sent each student a copy.

Students in my class talk about race and ethnicity in a way that many educators assume is impossible or too risky. Frank and honest dialogues about race are rare, so rare that a Web site (www.forum.com) has been created to let people learn about their differences in a safe, anonymous setting. This Web site has received a considerable amount of critical acclaim for fostering an open, honest dialogue about diversity and racial diversity in particular. However, it is possible to achieve this same kind of dialogue face-to-face. A good example is something I call the beanbag exercise.

The beanbag exercise takes place toward the end of the semester, since it requires a considerable amount of trust and openness. We sit in a tight circle, and I ask the students to share a story or comment they have heard about members of another racial or ethnic group. I usually start by citing an outlandish comment I heard in my youth, and then I throw the beanbag to a student who then shares his or her story. The stories run the gamut from touching and sad to funny, tragic, and provocative. Interestingly, many stories focus on subjects such as sex and hygiene—subjects that we think about but rarely talk about in an interracial setting. We then take a critical look at what was shared, whether the comments are stereotypical and why, and how we have been affected. The aim is to bring the explosive subjects of diversity and race out into the open and to reveal the misconceptions and misunderstandings that exist on all sides. For many of my students, it is the first time in their lives that they have shared and evaluated assumptions such as these in a racially integrated setting. The classroom, I believe, is our best opportunity to address issues such as these. If not the classroom, then where?

Throughout the semester, much of my teaching focuses on developing diversity consciousness—a deep-seated awareness and understanding that forms the foundation for the development of a variety of skills in the area of diversity. Drawing in large part on my experiences as a teacher, I describe six areas of diversity consciousness in my book, *Diversity Consciousness: Opening Our Minds to People, Cultures, and Opportunities* (2004).[2] These areas are:

Richard D. Bucher

- examining ourselves and our worlds
- expanding our knowledge of others and their worlds
- stepping outside of ourselves
- gauging the level of the playing field
- checking up on ourselves
- following through.

Intellectual and emotional growth in each of these areas requires that teaching be more than just an intellectual exercise. Rather, quality teaching requires a strong commitment and holistic change. In the process of opening myself up to my students, I am transformed by my students. Recently, I met with a number of focus groups made up entirely of students of color to discuss what faculty can do to promote their success. One theme that came up time and time again was the emotional and cultural distance between faculty and students. One student commented that instructors tend to work on their subject matter, not on themselves.

Over the years, I have facilitated numerous faculty development workshops dealing with diversity issues. Invariably, the discussion turns to multicultural activities, teaching techniques, and a variety of *do*s and *don't*s. While focusing on what we teach is important, it is only part of a continual, holistic process. It is equally if not more important for us to learn to step outside of ourselves and into the lives, histories, and cultures of our students. Moreover, quality teaching requires flexible thinking, struggling to understand our differences and similarities, continuing self-assessment, and practicing newly developed skills in the area of diversity.

A commitment to developing diversity consciousness needs to be a driving force in the pursuit of teaching excellence. We should continually seek to relate diversity to what we teach, how we teach, and whom we teach. As the cultural landscape continues to change dramatically, diversity is increasingly viewed as a bottom-line issue in fields ranging from business, government, and the military to health and education. While an increasingly diverse population of students can attain a quality education, we need diversity-conscious teachers to make that happen. Otherwise, the gap between student potential and achievement will continue to widen at all levels of education.

Notes

1. Richard Bucher, "Relationships, Success, and Community College Students of Color," in *Included in Sociology: Learning Climates That Cultivate Racial and Ethnic Diversity,* ed. Jeffrey Chin, Catherine White Berheide, and Dennis Rome (Washington, D.C.: American Association for Higher Education, 2002), 185–201.

2. Richard Bucher, *Diversity Consciousness: Opening Our Minds to People, Cultures, and Opportunities,* 2nd ed. (Upper Saddle River, N.J.: Pearson/Prentice Hall, 2004).

Paradoxical Pathways: A Feminist Teacher Treads Skillfully

Helena Meyer-Knapp

For a feminist teacher in America these can be thoroughly paradoxical times. At my college, the vast majority of students taking gender studies classes are women. So are the students who enroll in courses to explore whether or not to become teachers. Among the men in these classrooms, a substantial number publicly identify as gay and hence are unlikely to reach positions of power in public school education. In many school districts, by contrast, the superintendents are men, the majority of the high school principals are men, and the sport that still attracts by far the largest amount of media attention, school funding, and social attention is football—almost the only school sport for which there is no women's counterpart, not even one with poor attendance records and games that are scheduled at unattractive times.

My feminist mind starts to say that these are facts (or facts of life) in the politics of education that cry out for analysis and also cry out to be made visible. But then I stop, because I remember that each of these phenomena is eminently visible, and I remember that all too often when a woman poses questions about such issues directly, the surrounding community turns away muttering about how unhelpful it is to be "strident." These realities, in even more dramatic form, pervade my male-dominated core field, strategic studies, but more on that later. Even in a female-dominated field like education, at times it seems that nothing has changed. Older men still have disproportionate access to positions of power, and few young men seem interested in becoming skilled students of gender issues.

Yet these are very good times as well. Both as a scholar and as a teacher, I participate in a rich tradition of feminist work, which is getting stronger. The heritage for my own research into war and peacemaking spans back over fifty years to Simone Weil and Hannah Arendt, with more recent guidance from authors as disparate as Sarah Ruddick and Chandra Mohanty; the community of colleagues grows and grows. And the resources are just as rich for those thinking about teaching.

Elizabeth Minnich's groundbreaking book, *Transforming Knowledge*,[1] gives anyone who chooses to look wise guidance on ways to include the kinds of languages and systems of thought that have historically been marginalized in academic life. Minnich's work is only one part of a wide-ranging and creative conversation on teaching. From the rest of that discourse let me also single out bell hooks. Over the years, she has repeatedly pointed ahead down the feminist path to the next difficult topic. Recently she began asking college teachers to consider the bond between spiritual and scholarly discourse, a notion that is just as provocative in the new millennium as her first books on race in the university were over twenty years ago.

Women like hooks and Minnich have set out invaluable guideposts. I consider myself endowed with a series of sound pedagogical principles from which to work and with ready access to an enormous array of specifically feminist classroom resources online and in the bookstore. It is not hard to create a syllabus for any facet of my teaching when I need to illuminate the feminist and gender-related features of the subject at hand. If not the best of times, these are clearly pretty good times for feminist teachers.

Still it took me a number of years and quite a few mistakes to learn how to tread skillfully along these paradoxical pathways, neither deflected into giving up in distress by the relentlessness of the old ways nor losing contact with the realities that surround us by teaching only dreams about some utopian place. And since a teacher's life is made up of day-to-day choices—what to read, what to say and how to say it, how to evaluate, and what to modify for next time—learning how to tread these paths has meant learning how to make many different kinds of choices, and how to make them quickly.

With a new syllabus to design every term, and with evidence from the current semester that a particular book has failed to connect with the men though the women loved it, a teacher has to decide whether to reframe the chosen text with different lectures or to search for something new. The paradox, for those like me, is to teach effectively as a feminist in a setting that is not yet feminist and may never truly be so. My core strategies have been to be consistently transparent about what I am doing and to be inclusive of many voices.

Inclusiveness begins with the reading list, but the choice is more complex than simply opting for essays and books written by women. In most fields it is relatively easy to balance reputable male and female authors, but in addition I carefully examine the acknowledgements in a book or an article. I am interested in what authors have to tell me about the community in which they do their work, because their sex alone does not guarantee whether and how they will take up gendered aspects of their topic. I also try to ensure that the readings in their totality generate a dialogue among authors from different perspectives, the better to ensure that dialogue will then spread out into the class as a whole. Classic texts and authors have as important a place in a feminist classroom as in any other.

Since much popular writing in the United States, of the *Men Are from Mars, Women Are from Venus* variety, takes as its starting assumption that maleness and femaleness are innately, genetically different, I have opted to build cross-cultural analysis into most classes. When I teach courses about the politics of education, I compare Japan and the United States. Japan prioritizes academic content in middle school, at precisely the time when U.S. educators claim that sexuality and hormones prevent learning; this contrast allows my college-age students to engage gender issues and innateness while discussing national priorities and school curriculum. A comparison of the United States and Japan can open up discussions about innateness in relation to male violence as well, since contemporary Japan offers no evidence that young men are inherently physically violent. Cross-cultural analysis also makes it easier to focus students on the relationship between class and gender, since norms often vary widely across class lines.

Although I consider myself a feminist teacher, I do not insist that all my classes study gender. Still, feminism stays embedded in the manner in which I teach, no matter what I am teaching. For example, I am transparent when I challenge students to behave differently if class participation has become unbalanced with the men verbally dominant. And men still do tend to dominate discussion, even when they are in the minority numerically. However, whenever the imbalance starts to show itself, I rarely act on it until a few weeks into term, waiting until trust is strong enough that the issue can be raised directly. Then all I need to do is to ask the dominant speakers to pause before they speak, to open up enough time for others to jump in.

When I am team teaching, I make visible any topics over which my colleague and I may disagree, often to the surprise and delight of our students. For example, a philosopher lecturing on the derivation of a community's ethical principles who focuses exclusively on the Western tradition of logic and reason will find me making a comment from the back of the room about Confucian ethics and the importance of tradition and hierarchy in that world. While such moments risk encouraging already troubling student tendencies toward relativistic tolerance—the belief that there is no way to discern a legitimate ethical stance because we all have our own opinions—that, of course, is not my feminist purpose. I teach from the standpoint that discerning the nature of existing political realities often becomes easier after we have held a difficult dialogue across real differences.

Helena Meyer-Knapp

In addition, I tend to teach from example to theory and not the other way around. The semester's reading is likely to begin with a biography or a personal essay and go in to descriptive material; we take up abstract theoretical texts only midway through, once students have constructed a shared repertoire of stories and examples against which to test the theories. Furthermore, I use collaborative and exploratory projects and exercises. Students who craft a presentation collectively may be harder to grade as individuals, but they will have learned to care not only about their own work but also about their colleagues' endeavors. Students who are uncovering and inventing some of their own research strategies may not produce perfectly valid results, but they will have an indelible sense that designing a methodology entails a myriad of choices. If the research is to be sound, each choice must have a sound rationale. Ideally the rationale will include feminist concerns alongside the others.

As to evaluation—is there a feminist way to assign a grade? Here I owe the reader a confession. I teach at the Evergreen State College, where the transcript consists of student and faculty narrative evaluations of the student's work. Faculty and student meet to discuss those evaluations at the end of every term. While most college teachers consider this a radical format, in reality it does not differ much from the employee performance review that many of our students encounter in the workforce. Indeed most employers, male and female alike, agree that our students are exceptionally well prepared for the working world in this regard. This evaluation system, since it is collaborative and since it substitutes qualitative analysis for an absolutist and numerical standard, connects well with the model of teaching that I consider to be feminist. The very fact that interactive evaluation processes are unusual in college teaching may be a sign that colleges are "less" feminist in their assessment methodology than other workplaces.

Still, I have given grades in other teaching settings, and my experience suggests that there are more and less feminist ways to calculate a given student's grade. Grading on a curve, competitively, does not meet my feminist standards. It presumes that excellence is a rationed commodity and also that only a few outliers will be doing dreadful work. Neither of these assumptions stands up to close examination. Furthermore competitive grading systematically disadvantages those whose class and racial backgrounds are already underrepresented in college. Secondly, my grading policies ensure that a meaningful portion of the calculation is derived from qualitative as well as quantitative assessment mechanisms. While I might give some multiple-choice questions on an exam, I would also assign essays. While I would factor in homework grades, I would also assign value to classroom participation. This value cannot be laid out along a linear scale with more participation getting a higher grade. For some the required learning is to speak less and to offer space to those who are shyer about taking the floor; since there always are shyer students, a significant number of the participatory opportunities occur in small groups.

So these are teaching strategies that are useful across the array of liberal arts subjects I cover in our rather small college. Are these strictly feminist teaching strategies? Not in the sense that they are much more effective for women than for men, nor in the sense that they are designed to undermine an established canon in my field. But they are feminist in the sense that they resist the notion that there is a single universal truth and they resist the notion that it is my task as teacher to impose any such truth on others' minds. For readers who want to follow up on these issues, there is no better source than Minnich's *Transforming Knowledge* and her other more recent writings. She writes, for example:

> It is my conviction that students who leave classes
> practiced in thinking along with texts, teachers and a
> diverse sampling of other students are better off than
> those who leave with more content "in mind." I go for
> awakening interest and informing capacities over stock-
> ing minds in a world where storehouses are ever more
> accessible. . . . Independent, open minds that regard
> knowledge and skills as resources to be used for
> responsible purposes rather than possessions to
> be exploited for personal gain and power, remain
> all too rare.[2]

With such principles firmly set, why and how does a feminist modify her teaching? A vivid example of my own evolution comes from my earliest experiences teaching international studies, with a special focus on military and strategic studies. Those classroom encounters over fifteen years ago were often abrasive, confrontational, and difficult. Lectures on the core material from my doctorate, the military and strategic dimensions of the Cold War, were the worst. No sooner was I done than the young men in the audience opened up with hectoring questions of a kind I had not experienced in more general political studies courses. "Do you really think . . . ?" followed by some oversimplification of a complex notion I had been expounding. "How could you possibly say . . . ?" followed by a dismissive restatement of some "fact" of history to which my research was assigning a new meaning.

The questioning was clearly gendered; the sex of the speaker was all that was needed to give male students, young and old, veteran and peacenik alike, permission to challenge my credibility as an expert. This had not happened to

Helena Meyer-Knapp

me as a teacher before, perhaps because my degree from Oxford University and pronounced English accent had created an assumption of credibility. Suddenly that was gone. Still, the teaching challenge should not have been a surprise. My Cold War research was replete with evidence that even as late as the mid-1980s there were few women on the academic side of nuclear strategic studies; the serving military at the highest command levels was almost entirely male.

The lectures were a startling and disturbing experience. By then political studies was an arena in which women clearly had a voice. By moving over into military analysis, I had stepped over an invisible boundary, into the classrooms where the teachers are men, the students are mostly men, and a woman who walks to the front of the room must first establish her right to be heard at all. Furthermore, since my doctoral research included critical thinking about the Cold War and its portrayal in American political life, those on the more conservative end of the spectrum found additional grounds for suspicion. The surprise, of course, was the behavior of liberals. Even they found it hard to listen seriously to a woman.

And as a much more experienced college teacher in front of students who even now are sometimes prone to doubt my credibility, merely because I am a woman, I always need to be ready to take up the gender issues first. And surprisingly often I do. I talk about my gender and the factors that might impede my audience's hearing what I have to say about military strategy. Sometimes I start by asking the group to list quickly the criteria by which they assess credibility. As the list emerges: years of experience, recognition by outsiders, training, fieldwork, etc. I make my point by showing exactly where I meet and where I do not meet those criteria.[3] Once the gender conversations, which rarely need to last more than a few minutes, are in the open, the class can turn back to the official syllabus. Without such talk, a class session all too easily turns into a sad reminder of a feminist's "worst of times."

Yet these are also the best of times. At least at my college, most students are in search of an inclusive education, one that will enable them to work well in a highly diverse society. The problem is that sometimes the students themselves cannot guess in advance when they will have trouble hearing what a woman has to say. But *I* can guess that they will if the topic has anything to do with national security, and I remain willing again and again to help them hear about and see the world from a new and feminist standpoint. Nearly twenty years after I began work in the military wing of international relations, my paradoxical path keeps me exploring what must still be just about the most gender-divided field of study there is.

Notes

1. Elizabeth Kamark Minnich, *Transforming Knowledge* (Philadelphia: Temple University Press, 1990). New edition forthcoming.

2. Elizabeth Kamark Minnich, "Teaching Thinking: Moral and Political Considerations," *Change,* September/October 2003, 21.

3. During the George W. Bush administration, it has also been possible to deflect the conversation onto a comparison between the credibility of Secretary of State Colin Powell and that of National Security Advisor Condoleezza Rice. Students' initial assessments of Rice have routinely been profoundly dismissive. After such a conversation, they are at least willing to reopen the question of relative merits and look in a more serious way at the evidence.

Material Culture as a Window into the Social World

Linda B. Arthur

> I can't breathe, or think, and I don't have the energy to
> speak! I sit and watch the world go by and don't feel
> like I can be involved in it. I am no more than an
> observer of the social world that goes past my win-
> dow. And all because I have to wear a corset!
>
> —Student diary

Teaching about how culture and clothing intersect is an interesting way to approach social history. I teach a women's studies course called "Culture, Gender, and Appearance." In this course my goal is to have students understand how social norms are embedded in clothing and how clothing can come to constrain women's behavior. One of my students decided to do a large research project on the relationship between constraining social roles and the obvious constraint provided by corsets in the nineteenth century. After weeks of digging through numerous references, she didn't really understand the lived reality of how corsets controlled women's lives, so I gave her a reproduction of a historic corset to wear for two days. She kept a diary on her experiences; the quote above is one of her comments that led her to understand Naomi Wolf's obser- vations (in *The Beauty Myth*, 1992) that dress codes are less about clothing than about controlling women's behavior. I believe that there is no better way to bring home an idea than with hands-on experiences.

My philosophy on classroom instruction is simple: I want to stimulate my students' curiosity—I want them to always wonder about the *why* of human social behavior, especially as it pertains to the expression of ethnic identity in textiles and clothing. I fervently hope that my own curiosity about the connec- tions between culture and clothing is contagious. Stimulation of my students' critical thinking is my primary goal. I love teaching, and I want to share my enthusiasm with my students and, in the process, stimulate them to constantly wonder, question, and analyze everything they see. Through the exploration of cultural diversity in all of my classes, I hope to inspire the development of stu- dents' positive attitudes toward cultural relativity.

Relationships

Great professors touch students' lives both intellectually and personally. Their students come to see their professor as a person whose focus is to guide them toward their educational goals. Without that personal connection, I feel many students flounder in the setting of a large university. The foundation of good teaching is the development of a collaborative and caring relationship between professor and student that begins with the advising process, where a professor can get to know the students. It is important to have a sincere interest in the students' lives and goals and to be both approachable and available. Professors need to set clear personal boundaries, though, so that students understand that mentorship is not the same thing as friendship. I've found that if students call me by my first name, they see me as a friend and start to invite me to parties and clubs. Such a close relationship becomes problematic when it comes time to evaluate the student's work. To keep a professional distance, I always introduce myself on the first day of class as "Dr. Linda Boynton Arthur, but just call me Dr. Arthur." Mentorship continues after graduation. I still have regular contact with former students as I continue to provide career guidance—and they often continue to call me "Doc" for awhile.

Students need to feel that the professor is committed to their total education as a framework for their careers. A professor who treats students (and their time) with respect will demonstrate commitment to the cooperative educational process and in return garner respect from the students. Professors who are respected by their students can inspire students to achieve more than they thought they could; they will stretch when their professor shows faith and trust in them. One student gave me a memento that basically summarizes my philosophy; in a porcelain frame is the inspirational text, "To teach is to touch a life forever."

Course Content

I see myself not as a dispenser of wisdom but a facilitator of my student's learning. This philosophy is consistent with my teaching methods, which center on active learning that helps to make learning interesting and even fun. The first task is to get the students' attention, and the second is to keep the content interesting and relevant to what they already know and then either add to that knowledge or challenge it. I constantly aim for critical thinking. For example, I take a child's dress from the 1830s into the class when I introduce the topic of shifting gender norms. The dress is a boy's dress, which is identical to girls' dresses of the time period. Boys and girls parted their hair on different sides but otherwise dressed alike in the early nineteenth century. This example shows

Material Culture as a Window into the Social World

how to grab attention and challenge existing thought while inspiring critical thinking.

Motivating students is difficult at times and is more difficult when the professor is not attuned to students' varied needs and learning styles. After twenty years of teaching at the college level, I have seen a profound shift in the way students learn. While we've long known that different methods are good to use in the classroom, recently the time-honored lecture method has become less and less effective. Visual and kinesthetic methods are increasingly important to our students who have grown up in a media-saturated environment. Professors need to learn how to get students more involved. To that end, active learning, especially with much of the material delivered visually, has been a most useful strategy in my teaching.

Active Learning through Research

Dealing with an extremely diverse student population (we have no majority ethnic group) requires a flexible teaching strategy. A growing body of research today points to active learning strategies as a better way to cultivate critical thinking skills, engage students, and improve the quality of higher education; simply put, it is more interesting, relevant, and thought-provoking than the standard lecture format. I have used this method since I began teaching in the early 1970s. Strategies that I use in the classroom include use of audiovisual materials, discussion groups, outside speakers, experiential activities, fieldwork, and other types of primary research such as analysis of historic diaries, journals, and garments. I believe these active learning strategies make the course relevant, interesting, and involving and, in general, provide the students with a more satisfactory learning experience.

To prevent monotony, I find new ways either to deliver information or to facilitate active learning. At the very least, being open to unusual ways to inspire curiosity keeps the class lively and interested. I believe that my enthusiasm for the study of clothing and culture in general, and my research in particular, are transmitted to my students in such a way as to be contagious. This pays off in increased interest, motivation, and energy on the part of my students. Nothing delights me more than when a student comes to me with an unusual research idea; I want students to buy into the research process because this stimulates motivation.

Students need to find personal relevance in order for material presented in class to have meaning for them. The world is a social science lab, and if the professor is on the lookout for opportunities to bring real-world examples into the classroom, students find salient connections. Even tragedies provide fertile ground for teaching, because we must learn from the world's horrors. In the fall

Linda B. Arthur

semester of 2001 I was teaching a course on the cultures and costumes of South and Southeast Asia, and we had just covered Islamic philosophy with regard to gender and clothing regulations for women before the terrorist attacks on September 11. We woke up that morning to the news that the twin towers of New York City's World Trade Center had been attacked. Even though many professors cancelled classes that day, I went forward with my original lesson plan to continue a discussion of Islamic regulations. The discussion was all the more real during class on that day as we discussed the ethnocentrism of the United States, the hegemony of the Taliban, and other issues of culture and conflict. We went through with the original plan of having an Islamic scholar visit class to talk about Islam and gender roles in South Asia. Although this could have been a difficult situation for all involved, as a result of our prior discussion of ethnocentrism and cultural relativity, he was treated with courtesy and respect, in spite of the high emotions we all felt during that week.

The interaction of culture and clothing has always fascinated me, especially the overlap between ideology and clothing. As a result I have conducted a large body of research and published numerous articles and books related to these areas. That research becomes vital to my classroom teaching; students have a hand in the data collection and are most interested in the research process as a result. Because I believe that active learning is a more appropriate teaching methodology for costume classes, I introduce as many hands-on activities into the classroom as possible. For instance, costumes are brought into class and examined for both design and construction. In discussing the relationship between clothing and behavior, I show students an actual nineteenth-century corset. To help students see how the corset restricted breathing, I have a reproduction corset that students take turns wearing during the class. In addition, I constantly bring the historical and cultural aspects into contemporary perspective. Admittedly, mine is a somewhat unusual specialization, and while this could lead some scholars into obscurity, in my case the rarity of the topic, coupled with my ethnographic fieldwork, has yielded greater visibility.

Management Techniques

Each class session has a specific set of goals and activities. I begin each class with a quick summary of the last so that the key points are made clear. The syllabus has a schedule of topics and daily readings. Changes are agreed upon in advance so the students can make any necessary alterations to their own schedules. Because most of our students work at least half time while attending the university, they appreciate that I use their time to the best advantage.

The syllabus should be seen as a contract between professor and student; it should lay out policies clearly and specify the point value of projects and the grading scale for the class. Fairness and objectivity are necessary to build trust, and to that end the use of evaluation forms and grading rubrics, shared in advance with the students, allows them to see how their work will be judged.

Constant feedback is important. Many of my classes are writing-intensive, so we spend a great deal of time crafting written projects. A paper is written, critiqued, rewritten, and then graded. Examples of good work need to be provided for reference. Students especially appreciate feedback regarding their grades. After each test or major project, I let each student know how they're doing in the class at that moment by passing around my grading sheet (without names, only social security numbers). This way we can find out if any projects haven't been graded or if the grade was incorrectly reported.

Specific instructions for papers and projects are necessary. On one exam I wrote an essay question that read, "Show how shifting gender roles were seen in nineteenth-century dress, and use examples for illustration." A fair portion of the responses were pencil drawings. The point I am trying to make here is that professors need to think critically as well and to try to read instructions as the student might.

In sum, students are more involved and engaged in the educational process when the information provided is meaningful, relevant, and interesting. When a good mentoring relationship is established, the students are more likely to be successful in achieving their educational goals. It all begins with a good collaborative relationship between professor and student.

The Education of a Professor

David Louzecky

I really must admit to a bit of disappointment. There I was, much younger, a recent Ph.D., brimming with enthusiasm, ready for energetic professional engagement. There I was, the one philosopher on a two-year campus in the hinterlands—not exactly what I had foreseen in my "vision thing." I must also admit to being grateful to have found a job doing what I really wanted to do.

Two senior professors sat me down and explained the University of Wisconsin–Sheboygan's open-door policy and emphasis on quality teaching. So I propped open my office door, set aside my work on analytic epistemology, and devoted myself to teaching and talking with students. Almost immediately it became apparent that my narrow technical training, excellent though it was for research and publication, had not prepared me to teach introductory freshman and sophomore courses.

I immediately began the education of a professor: I returned to the great perennial problems that had drawn me to philosophy in the first place, began browsing the classics, and read widely—very widely—in an effort to connect philosophy to the interests of students. The more widely I read, the more I discovered philosophy—everywhere. *Hmm.* Perhaps it is better to lay the technical foundations in graduate school and add breadth later; it is the emphasis on teaching in the University of Wisconsin Colleges that has allowed me to do just that. Becoming a good teacher as well as becoming a philosopher in the grand old tradition of Socrates completely outweighs the resultant slower pace of my technical work.

The excitement of my own education was contagious in the classroom and more than compensated for my early lack of polished presentation. In fact, I noticed that as I became more polished, my students became less engaged. There were more notes to take and fewer opportunities to challenge and explore. Perhaps the truly great professor would be so polished that such openings would just appear, but that seems to me to be too much of a performance.

In *The End of Education* Neil Postman suggests teaching occasionally in a completely different field. Perhaps that's a bit extreme, and it certainly wouldn't be allowed in our rigid institutions. But we can introduce into our courses topics that are new to us, that we don't know much about. We'll get to learn with our students, share their anxiety about "not knowing it all," and be less likely to lecture than to inquire. It works, perhaps not so well for those new at teaching, but for those of us who have had enough success to have enough confidence to fumble and say, "I don't know; let's both try to find out." Gaining information from a well-prepared lecture is valuable; so is learning how to explore new ideas by joining with a professor. Just as students need to learn the content of our fields, they need to learn the techniques of inquiry.

Often my enthusiasm outstrips the mutual abilities of my students and me. Once, I tried to teach epistemology using the "possible-worlds" semantic interpretation of modal logic. I would laugh now at the hubris of the attempt if my poor students hadn't struggled so hard. I'm sure they learned a great deal, but it was labor without even a glimmer of enjoyment. I should have recognized this early and modified the course, but it's a lot harder to say, "I made a big mistake in developing this course," than it is to say, "I don't know the answer to this question." Unless we allow for modifications, however, we run the risk of losing our students' hearts and minds. To help avoid this mistake I always label the assignment sheet "tentative" and consider the semester a failure if there aren't some changes.

I have continued my education, and as I encounter interesting ideas, articles, and books, I incorporate them into my classes. Although doing so requires major changes every semester, my own interest has never waned, and that interest, attached to the great ideas, rarely fails to engage students. Too many changes, however, can be exhausting for both students and professor.

Quite often students ask such insightful questions that it's necessary to reflect not on my feet but in the quiet of my office and work up an entirely new lecture-discussion for the next class. Twice I've tried, not entirely successfully, to conduct an entire course on the basis of guided responses, a tutorial writ large. But this doesn't work when forced. I like this practice a lot; students don't. It has too little structure for them. Even when I explain how everything hangs together, they remain anxious. I've even tried not handing out a syllabus but had to relent to quell the panic. In any case, I'm grateful that they refuse to allow that method, for it takes far more time and energy than is allowed by my college's teaching and governance load. Taking a few class periods to respond thoroughly to particularly interesting questions seems to work rather well. At least the students tolerate it, and I enjoy it. It's far too easy to simply blame students and their poor preparation for the lack of success of this method, for it requires a felicitous mix of students, professor, and ideas. When it happens, however, there is no better teaching. In an effort to keep both students and myself flexible and open to questions and exploration, I delete the dates from my syllabi and try not to worry too much about "getting through the material." The "yin" of change and response is engagement of both students and professor.

The "yang" is that it can expand to consume most of a professor's time. Good teaching in any case, and especially with an open door, expands to absorb all of one's time and energy.

The longer I teach, the more I'm convinced that character is more important than technique. That most students are not well prepared for college-level work, at least outside of the elite institutions, should be viewed as a challenge for teaching, not an excuse for bashing. Condescension has no place in the classroom. Students recognize their ignorance; that's one reason they come to college in the first place, and they are willing to work exceedingly hard if they recognize the value of the enterprise. As with teaching course material, explaining its value must be done in a way that connects with their present knowledge and interests.

One of my most rewarding experiences occurred when I spent several semesters teaching at a nearby correctional facility. Prisoners know well both senses of the word *con*. All around them they see other cons like themselves, and they constantly are aware of and participate in various cons—posturings and exaggerations and deals—that are part of everyday prison life. In this milieu it was refreshing to find that the students were eager to learn, and at the same time were impatient with anything that didn't ring true. On the first day of class several had all the books read and asked questions about material at the end of the course—to see if I was prepared. They would have been all over me if I had tried to stuff them with facts or ideas without any evidence to back it up. I learned this from rough experience, but I also found that the inmates were ready and eager to learn, as they had not been able or willing to learn on the "outside."

Among my students at the prison was Jim, who after reading Kant, decided not to enroll in the drug therapy program. The program would have reduced his sentence, but he found the manipulative aspects insulting. Jim thought he would have a better chance of staying clean and living well if he focused on Kantian dignity and responsibility. The right decision? Maybe, maybe not. But he understood his role as a moral agent. The decision was his to make.

One of my colleagues keeps pressing me for the "nuts and bolts" of good teaching. I have neither. I'm fortunate to be in a field filled with ideas that most everyone finds initially interesting and often important. My task is to extend and deepen students' knowledge without obliterating their interest. For most philosophers, I suspect, the interest in the technical problems is generated by their connections with fundamental issues in religion, morality, politics, and science. These connections need to be made with some care. When they are, students have little difficulty enduring a fair amount of intellectual complexity.

At the beginning of every semester, another colleague comes by to tell me that my students would do even better if I would require their attendance in

David Louzecky

class. I agree, but I can't take attendance because it's disrespectful. He rolls his eyes and leaves to prepare his seating chart. Students have a right to decide whether to attend class, and their responsibility should not be evaded by the impositions of an authority.

It's easy to see that I'm correct. Although my institution is at the bottom of the status hierarchy, it has some interesting features. For example, about half of my students are over twenty-five. Parents aren't dictating to them. They don't live at home or in dorms. They've made some choices about their lives; they have jobs and families and full lives away from the campus. Can you imagine my asking the thirty-year-old engineer, the forty-year-old librarian, the fifty-year-old farmer, the sixty-year-old attorney, or the seventy-year-old retiree for an excuse for their absence? Can you imagine requiring them to reveal their business, family, or medical problems? That's an invasion of privacy for which none of them would stand. Eighteen-year-olds are recent adults, inexperienced and vulnerable, but they deserve the same respect. I would also argue that requiring students to make choices and accept responsibility has good consequences in preparing them for the "real" world.

We should all be able to remember being in the same position as our students—unable to mobilize effort because we wondered whether it was worthwhile, unable to ask helpful questions because of pervasive confusion, unable to concentrate because of raging hormones. And most of my students have to hold down jobs that sap much of their time and energy.

Sometimes students come to our campus after failing at larger institutions. They've partied too much, or they haven't been equipped to deal with academic rigor, or they've needed more support from friends and family. Larry is such a student. He "flunked out" from the four-year flagship campus at Madison and came home with his tail between his legs. He got a job in a factory but found it dull, dirty, and generally unpleasant. So he decided to try a course at our campus. It was a history survey. He enjoyed history and did reasonably well, so Larry decided to try some other courses. One of them was introductory philosophy. Being smart but not yet completely grown-up, he oscillated between active participation and a detachment born partly of fatigue from juggling his job and a couple of courses. Larry eventually decided, with the support of his parents and some student loans, to come back to school full time, majoring in history.

Why is Larry a philosophy success story? One day soon after he decided to quit his job for school, he stopped by my office and thanked me. He told me that philosophy taught him to think harder about his life, to decide what he wanted to do instead of just drifting along. I don't tell this anecdote to suggest what a great teacher I am. I simply believe that as a side effect of treating students with

The Education of a Professor

respect and talking about ethical issues they become aware of themselves as moral agents, with an ability to make decisions about their lives.

As I've mentioned previously, many of my students are older than the typical eighteen- through twenty-some-year-olds. Sue was one of them, a forty-five-year-old who kicked out her husband after one too many of his alcoholic binges. Sue was quiet. She did well on exams and papers but didn't participate very much in class. She listened, though. And sometimes she stopped by my office and the offices of my colleagues. It turned out that she was simply shy, feeling that she didn't belong, even in classes where fully half the students were no longer youngsters. We all told her that she should not be reluctant to speak up, and at the same time we listened, listened to her ideas and insights. Sue had a seemingly peculiar aspiration for someone of her age and background: she wanted to become a sociology professor. A daunting goal. She knew she needed to complete lots of coursework and many years of study.

Little by little Sue opened up in class. She saw that her professors weren't indifferent to her ideas, and neither were the other students. Sue took all of the courses on our campus that she could and completed an associate's degree. She has moved on to a bigger campus and is pursuing her dream.

Why did Sue thrive on our small campus? Because her professors and fellow students listened and took her ideas seriously. Listening to students is important. Genuinely listening. Too often we're in a hurry to cover the syllabus or attack the stack of reports on our desks. Too often students are shy in asking, like Sue, and diffident in re-asking, when surrounded by peers. We must not merely say, we must make it clear, that there is time, both inside and outside of class, to pursue students' questions as part of an exchange that results in understanding. Sometimes all this listening requires burning the midnight oil, the balm that turns a job into a vocation. Though it's exhausting, devoting time and energy to students has its reward.

Too many students are disengaged from what they are doing. They sign up for courses not because they desire insight, inspiration, or skills or because of any inherent interest in the topics, but because the courses fit into the complex matrices of requirements for their majors or their degrees or because the courses are being offered at convenient times. Colleges and universities are not blameless in this matter. To an increasing degree, they pander to this focus upon the externals. Our degree requirements are Byzantine, and our advertisements give prominence to the financial rewards. We spend too much time tailoring programs to jobs and too little time on how to live a good life and create a good society.

Both individually and socially habits are important and good habits matter even more so. Initially others instill these habits in us through socialization, indoctrination, and education. There comes a time, however, when individuals need to take control of their own lives, to become responsible not just for their habits but also for their goals and aspirations. Otherwise, they exist as mere social products and are not truly autonomous. Taking control requires the rational examination of one's life, which can only be done in the context of freedom. This is where a college education can offer something significantly different from anything that might have been experienced in secondary education or that will occur in the business world. It can give students, especially those who have just come of age, an opportunity to reflect on what ends, what endeavors, they wish to pursue and to determine whether their present habits, their present characters, are suited for these purposes. They can reflect upon the nature of the good life.

Philosophy courses are ideally suited to play a pivotal role in this educational process. Not only is living well at the center of student interest, it is at the center of philosophy. Although hormones and conventions drive a great deal of student behavior, students, like everyone else, have an interest in flourishing. A philosophy class can be especially beneficial in giving students a time, a place, and an incentive to reflect on what life should really be about. Philosophy courses can provide students with something they sorely need: opportunities to reflect rationally on the life choices they are in the process of making.

Of course my students at the correctional facility had already made many unfortunate choices. But the ones who make it into the classroom are primed to change. Eric was in prison for car theft, and as a juvenile he had had earlier brushes with the law. One day he told me he was reading John Rawls's *A Theory of Justice*. I tried to talk him out of it because it is difficult and dull, and I suggested some philosophical reading material that I said would be more fun. Eric replied that he had already had plenty of fun. Fun was one of the reasons he was in prison, and he wanted to do something important. Perhaps Rawls wasn't such a bad choice after all. I have no idea where Eric or Jim are today or what they are doing. But I am proud that whatever choices they made after our class began with the understanding that they had at least some power to change their lives, for better or for worse.

Teaching is a collaborative activity. Lectures and labs have their place in the learning environment, but teaching at its best is an exchange among people engaged in genuine inquiry. Although I began my career as a lecturer, I gradually learned to trim the lecturing and to prompt students to ask questions, a Socratic method in reverse. While attempting to answer their questions, I learned to ask questions of my own, questions that are puzzling and fruitful. Too often, the Socratic method is a stern quiz on assigned material or a lecture disguised as questions. But if we keep our course material fresh and continue to find the world filled with wonder, then the classroom will be a place to collaborate in coming to understand ourselves in our world.

The collaborative enterprise that I began in the classroom with students soon included colleagues. After lengthy discussions of teaching, a political scientist and I wrote a book, *The Good Life: Personal and Public Choices,* to be used as an introduction to ethics and social policy. We continued our collaboration by designing and team-teaching a course, "Feminism, Equality, and Public Policy." Presently, we are connecting a social philosophy course with a political science course in a "learning community." The two courses are run back-to-back, essentially combined into one big course. We are both in the classroom, and instead of taking turns teaching, we join in discussion with students. For several years, a sociologist and I did a weekly cocurricular "point—counterpoint" session on ethics, religion, and social issues. We continued these sessions as participants in a new curricular offering, "Freshman Forum." Early in these sessions I realized that students had a lively interest in personal ethics, and I collaborated with a librarian in designing and teaching a new course, "Moral Issues in Personal Life: Friends and Others." Collaboration involves learning with and from others and should become a way of life as well as a way of teaching.

Instructional technology provides both opportunities and challenges for those interested in collaborative learning. There are thirteen U.W. Colleges. Because the philosophy department is geographically dispersed, technology is essential, and we have become far more proficient in its use than departments in which colleagues are clustered in adjacent offices. We are now thinking about ways to use technology to invite each other into our classrooms. It would enhance our classes and engage our students, especially on one-philosopher campuses, to be able to have active exchanges with other philosophers via the Web. A group of campus colleagues—a scientist, social scientist, musician, and I—designed and taught a capstone course, "Using the Internet: Ethics, Politics, and Aesthetics."

I want to introduce my students to philosophy; I want them to make its acquaintance and join the "conversation of humankind." Since I hope this introductory meeting interests them, my second goal is to create the sort of classroom engagement that prompts students to seek out and enjoy philosophical encounters outside the classroom. My aim is to help them understand the importance of philosophy and to use what they've learned to reflect profitably on their personal and public lives.

What I have already accomplished is particularly gratifying because I'm a severe stutterer. Why on earth would a stutterer choose a talking career? My explanations tend toward the mundane. Early I was attracted to the big philosophical questions—God, value, freedom—and later to the more technical

David Louzecky

problems on which their resolution depends. Still later I was attracted to the sort of organization and clarity required for effective classroom presentation—so attracted, in fact, that facing the difficulties of speaking seemed worth the try. My first few experiences as a teaching assistant were, if not as good as I hoped, at least better than I feared—good enough, in fact, to try again. Because the research professors under whom I worked were serious about quality teaching, it must have taken considerable courage to let me into a classroom. My accomplishment has been aided in no small part by students and colleagues who have extended patience and consideration, returning a hundredfold the respect I show to them.

The very best classes are those in which students actively take over the conversation with passionate engagement—and this can happen only in an environment of respectful and fair collaboration. Since my classes always fill to capacity, I've had a large number of students, and over the years I've received many visits and letters from former students indicating that their courses in philosophy have been an enormous help in advanced college work and in their personal and public lives. They've learned to think for themselves and to do that more clearly and responsibly. Of late I've had former students stop by to tell me that they are recommending my classes to their own college-age children. In a career that I consider only half over, there can be no greater testimony of success. Recently the university informed me that I am eligible for retirement. I was shocked because I hadn't given it a thought, but when the dean came by to ask when I was planning to retire, I was ready with an answer: I have no such plans. I took up philosophy and teaching not because there were no other career opportunities but because I had a passion for both. I still do.

So I really must admit to a bit of elation. Here I am, much older, without a diminution of enthusiasm, actually engaged in the work that constitutes my life. Suppose I had found the position I envisioned. My early work indicates that I could have achieved at least a moderate professional standing. But in responding to the standards of the profession it is unlikely that I would have worked so hard at teaching or read so widely or considered connections so carefully, activities that have lead to the comprehensiveness of view necessary to move beyond the confines of the merely professional. Here I am, feeling like a philosophy professor. Here I am, happier than I otherwise would have been. Here I am, living what I take far more than a professional interest in: the good life.[1]

Note

1. I would like to thank Lynn Gordon and Tom Zillner for helpful comments. Some of the ideas are borrowed from "Can Virtue Be Taught (and If So, Should It Be Taught?)," which was delivered by my coauthor, Roger Rigterink, at the Twenty-Third Conference on Value Inquiry.

Note to Self: A Member of the "Backpacked and Briefcased" Shares the Reminders That Keep Him Going

James "Bucky" Carter

When first approached about writing an essay for this publication, I was a little overwhelmed—*and scared.* I knew that my words would be in close proximity to a Nobel Prize recipient's and surrounded by those whose years of teaching experience and accolades far eclipse my few years and honors. Yet one idea that runs throughout this work is that of being a lifelong learner, one who is both a teacher and a student. I am certainly that, literally and philosophically, and I believe it gives me a unique insight into this project.

I have for most of my life as an educator always been the student/teacher, one of the "backpacked and briefcased," as I like to call it, referring to the accoutrements folks in my situation and I are often found in simultaneous possession as one who is taking classes while teaching his own, learning the ropes while helping others do the same. I know I don't have all the answers to successful teaching yet, nor do I have the particular aged ethos of others in the pages bordering and beyond mine, but, since I am used to being in this liminal space, this area between established teachers even as I move toward becoming one myself, I believe my own ethos as one of the "backpacked and briefcased" is pertinent in that it perfectly illustrates multiple roles of a lifelong learner.

I am not completely without teaching experience, though. As a North Carolina Teaching Fellow, a member of one of the nation's most-renowned programs that gives high school seniors full tuition to college and specialized training in exchange for four years of service teaching in public schools, I have been in and out of schools as an instructor since my sophomore year in college. I have seen good teachers, bad teachers, innovators, and total bores. After I finished my student teaching by being named an Outstanding Prospective Teacher, I landed my first "gig" teaching high school English to tenth graders and remedial readers and learned all the joys and pains of dealing with excellent educators, administrators, and supporting staffs as well as not-so-stellar representatives thereof.

Now, as I am taking graduate classes toward an M.A. and teaching freshman composition classes at the University of Tennessee, I am aware that I have already seen a wide spectrum of educational theories, practices, and methodologies and all spectrums of success among them. I am, as are many teachers, a gatherer of ideas (a downright thief of many!) and an amalgamation of all that I have seen and tried to copy or promised myself never to do. In many ways, the beginning teacher is the epitome of all teachers. We recognize more than most the mounting hill of knowledge we have yet to climb, the mysterious situations looming on the horizon, and perhaps worst of all, that there are challenges coming our way for which we cannot possibly be prepared. This is the situation we all find ourselves in right before we step into a classroom, really; it's just that we newbies still have classes of our own to take and teachers of our own to challenge.

Being a "newbie" teacher at the university, of course, I sometimes have to remind myself of what I've found to work best for me. One early lesson I believe all educators must learn is that teaching is as individual as the people who teach. What one person does, another may not be able to pull off successfully. Further, as we learn from our experience, we sometimes forget that the lesson isn't really learned if one can't apply the knowledge. Following are a number of things I must retell myself every so often, whether it be at the beginning of a new semester or while within the throes of day-to-day teaching. I ask that if you find something useful, feel free to assimilate it. I certainly have stolen from my neighbors in this collection, and odds are if I ever see you teach, I'll steal from you, too. On the other hand, if you are one of the outstanding educators to have conquered all the challenges I am still presented with and feel that your lifelong learning process is pretty much at its end, please forgive me as I growl at you from beneath this page, a lot disappointed and a little jealous, but know I appreciate your time reading my essay, appreciate your feedback, no matter what it be, am smiling at you to your face, and look forward to seeing you again soon. I am, after all, still a backpacked graduate student, you know, and can smile to your face while growling underneath.

At the beginning of each semester, my first reminder is often "Bucky, be quick!" This is shorthand for what I tell myself before every new class, when I find myself nauseous, nervous, and trying my best to be just a little bit intimidating (not easy for a baby-faced, pudgy young man of less than six feet, I assure you!). For the first fifteen minutes or so I look out at a sea of usually blank faces and just know they are waiting for me to turn my back so, like nonchalant wolves, they can devour me. Yet I know it is my role to set the rules and expectations from the get-go. It is I who need, in these early days, to have the eye of the predator. "Bucky, especially if you see yourself as an authoritarian type of teacher"—which is what I've fooled myself into thinking I am at times—"this simple step now can help save headaches down the road when students are more likely to call you out because of ambiguous requirements, policies, and the like. Even though they may be on your syllabus, the one you spent three whole days typing out and editing and reediting, *reiterate your rules; make them accept them as their own!"*

This reminder, or shorter, more expletive-laden derivatives, depending on how much I'm panicking, is my lifeline in those scary first moments. Also, when making classroom regulations and policy I try to remember to do two things: *Be clear. Be concise.* A third rule of thumb I follow after the rules have been set, and I feel less like my perspiration is appearing to my students as a nice gravy sauce, is to *be consistent.* We all know that extenuating circumstances come up and that classroom regulations are somewhat fluid, but there are ways to make sure students do not miss two weeks worth of class attending the funerals of fifteen different grandparents. "Bucky, be quick"—quick on my feet, quick in my head, quick to establish my own presence, and quick to hide the initial fear I know they can smell.

Another thing that I had to remind myself of in the very earliest days of my teaching career, back when I was still an undergraduate and only a student observer in local classrooms, was to move around! Luckily, this is one I learned quickly, being naturally fidgety. When I was in my first few months of employment as a high school English teacher, I would often come home dead tired. Fresh out of undergraduate school, I was living with my mother at the time, and one day, upon noticing my exhausted frame, she remarked, "Yeah, sometimes sitting down all day can be just as tiring as being on your feet." My remark was a swift, "Sitting down? I hardly ever get a chance to sit down!" Of course, my mother was remembering an older model of high school teacher, the kind she had in the seventies, and, I suppose, the kind that hardly ever budged. Yet that old, staid model of teacher seems to make somewhat of a comeback in the college classroom, especially in the graduate course.

As simple a reminder as it is, I recommend to myself and to all teachers that, if space allows it, we spend some time being kinetic. I try to remember the old "Power T" research that says that most of the best students usually sit in the front row or down the middle of the room. Why not change the "T" around by walking to different points in the room? Though I may have just come from a two-hour-long seminar where my professor only moved once, and then only to catch a better glimpse of a buxom colleague, I must constantly remind myself that students at the high school level and the undergraduate level need more pizzazz, more energy to keep them with me as I lead them along the day's adventures in learning.

I suppose, also, that my proclivity toward movement might also relate to that first primal fear I spoke of in the preceding paragraphs. There may be a part of me that sublimates that now-repressed fear, telling my subconscious, "If you're

James "Bucky" Carter

on your feet constantly, little backpacked and briefcased bunny, they might not catch you so easily!" I would like to think, however, that classroom movement is one of those things that I have internalized on my own rather than failed to recognize as instinct, and I'd appreciate it if you would allow me to continue to think so. The up side to the Freudian analysis, though, is that it helps me through those two-hour seminars. There's nothing quite like staring at a Yeats or James scholar and seeing a rabbit just too uninteresting to eat.

Along with movement, I must remember to practice proximity, one of the most underused but most enjoyable, subversive strategies ever to come out of a teacher-training class! Yet another reason to move around in class, proximity is a powerful, sneaky tool that all teachers at every level can use. Though one hopes not in upper-level classes, in many freshman English classes I've found that the format is not exactly one that supports an innately high level of interest among students. It is not uncommon to see students get sidetracked with their own conversations in these classes, even in the most riveting of situations, or even when the instructor is talking (i.e., *when I'm dangling some meat in front of them but they'd rather chew on other things*).

At the University of Tennessee, graduate teaching associates refer to something called the "Glocker factor." The Glocker building is an older structure furnished with more tables than desks, more columns than rows. The classrooms within are truly formidable teaching antagonists.

Having taught in a recently renovated building in my first semester of independent teaching at the University of Tennessee, I was spoiled. My classroom was a new "smart classroom" complete with aerodynamic plastic desks (just in case a student decided to fly away); a nice, sleek screen that unfurled itself at my command; and a media station where I could easily show videos from an overhead LCD or get Internet access right then and there—and the station commands were all integrated into my podium! In my second semester, though, I was assigned to Glocker 205. It is right next to a busy street, has a painted piece of cardboard nailed into the wall instead of a screen, and has an old-fashioned wooden podium that I couldn't use because it sat on one of those old 1950s (I'm being generous in my dating) chemistry tables and hence was too high up for someone of my short stature—unless I wanted to use sock puppets to help me teach, that is. All in all, if my former classroom was a "smart classroom" this one easily qualified for special education.

It is a given among teachers in Glocker that, among the diverse other problems, students who sit at the back tables or desks—if you are lucky enough to have a classroom with desks!—will inevitably tune out or decide to chat independently of the lecture. Having taught in Glocker myself briefly the year before and utilized this old teacher trick of proximity from my days as a high school teacher, I've been able to cut down on that incessant buzz in order to ignore other problems the building imposes that I cannot do anything about.

How so? Most college students—and most people in general in our culture—automatically become more reserved and quiet as an unknown person or authority figure moves closer to them, crowding their personal space. Further, freshmen in particular seem to have a fear of being rude to their professors, or at least of being called out at being rude to them. By simply walking to the back of the room in Glocker, or nearby someone who might be off task, I can usually silence the chatter, awake the slumbering intellectual giant, or give any other sort of pressure-filled, silent, and uncomfortable enforcer of my will, allowing my own marvelous words to be exactly where they ought to be when I'm talking: at the fore of my students' attentions.

Now, there is certainly an ideology among collegiate teachers that says that disciplining is "not what we do." But proximity is just subversive enough for the practitioner not to have to give up anything within that ideology and just sneaky enough for college professors, whom I've found to be, as a group, more than eager to feel like they are getting away with something. (Who's to say that the student knows you've moved closer to him or her for a reason? In fact, the object is to do it and never let them know you are doing it.) I remind myself to utilize proximity often, and I suggest you try it too. I guarantee it to work—in most cases. In fact, try it the next time you're at a faculty meeting. Sit closest to the person who regularly pisses you off. When he or she begins to do so, lean in real close. Who's the bunny now, baby?

I must within my next self-reminder share with you that this is one that I very, very often forget. It is very simple: "Inculcate technology, Bucky!" English faculties in particular seem to be the most resistant to jumping on the technology bandwagon, probably because any use of technology outside of the copier or a video has the potential to be more of a hassle or disaster than our tried-and-true methods of lecture and discussion, and even the copier isn't always reliable. And, honestly now, how many times have *you* seen a PowerPoint presentation go sour at the worst possible time? Yes, it happens, but teachers must realize that every one of the students with whom they come into contact will be affected by technology. E-mail communications and list serves are fairly simple to set up, and many universities have specialists to help get them going. I do my very best to experiment with some form of multimedia at least once a semester. I know that if I don't feel comfortable doing it, I can probably get the students to help. Many are coming to the university now with more computer skills than most senior faculty, you know.

Further, early exposure to technologies that students are less likely to have had before coming to school, like academic databases, PowerPoint, and LCDs, can truly help freshmen see firsthand how communication and presentation are changing in our technocentric global society. The English department is not immune to this change, though we may constitute the most resistant faction on campus. In fact, I know of a handful of innovative Ph.D. programs that will now allow students to substitute one foreign language with computer competence, encouraging students to stay on top of the transformation that is slowly but surely seeping into English departments nationwide. As hard as it can be, I want to use technology in my classroom and ask that all teachers in all departments always be looking for ways to use it in theirs.

As my motivation, I think of the hypothetical instance of a poor student who, from some odd stroke of fate, has had three years worth of classes in a building like Glocker. The sad sack will hardly know what clothes are in fashion, much less have the technological skills he or she might need to be a functioning, college-educated member of society! Not unless, that is, I make an effort.

Now for something I love reminding myself to do: "Try small group activities, Bucky!" There is the notion among some college-level teachers that any minute not spent in lecture or full-class discussion is a minute wasted, a minute of neglecting the financial end of the student-teacher contract that says that the parents, state, banks, and students paid for so many minutes of intense instruction. Oh the pressure!

"Note to self: group time *is* class time—if handled properly." There are two major tips I review while planning such activities: 1. "Five, alive"—keep groups no larger than five members. 2. "Show me now"—have the groups produce some sort of "accountability," a list of the ideas they had, some short write-up to turn in, a short presentation on what they discussed or worked on, for example, and have this "accountability" be necessary to the class discussion for the day and to be used directly after the small groups have met.

In other words, I strive to make the accountability immediate. I have found that having the groups turn in their accountability the next class period or after a long weekend diffuses the sort of "hustle" mentality and intense focus the small group should have. Small group activities work great when handled effectively and can also really help to flesh out a lesson plan or class period, especially a class session that runs longer than sixty minutes. Plus, they're just plain fun, whether one is listening to the groups plan or using proximity to make sure the groups are staying on task!

Here is a reminder that, in contrast to the one above, is not always so fun: "Know that no matter how good you are at teaching, there is always something that can be improved upon, something that you may not even be aware that you do." No one likes to be told he or she is doing poorly, especially when he or she knows the intense effort being put into a situation, but odds are that even you veterans have some area in which you can develop further. For example, you may favor one side of the room more than another, looking at the left for most of your lecture, for instance. Or perhaps, despite all the articles and books you've written in women's lit and women's studies and your Berkeley- or Brown-educated enlightenment about gender equality, you may do what most teachers unconsciously do: call on more males than females.

This self-reminder, though usually followed by a bit of self-berating on my part, especially when I find something I tried to fix before, is most important because it reminds us that teaching is fluid and evolutionary. It is like writing and reading and grading and staying awake during department meetings: the more you do it, the better you get at it. Many of us have a fear of being evaluated by our peers because we see our teaching as something rather personal. There are ways to get over this, though. Why not set up a video camera and evaluate yourself? That's one of the things I do. And when observers offer information on things they noticed, keep in mind what was stated earlier: there is always something that can be improved on—and maybe those folks will help you see what you can't see when teaching. Of course, someone will inevitably say something that you know not to be true. In those instances, return with me to your days as a graduate student, to times of yore when you just received a poor mark on a paper and the professor called you in to tell you all about it. Smile, nod, and walk away.

I find that my reminders often fall into two categories: the practical pedagogical and the ideological. Proximity, my thoughts on small group activities and improvement—these are of the practical sort, of course, but there a few reminders that might be even more important to me, and these are often of the ideological kind.

Here is one of the most important: "Keep the parachutes open, Bucky!" Surely you've seen the bumper stickers that read, "Minds are like parachutes; they only work when open." A good teacher should take that to heart. A number of good changes have come from our nation's move toward being more sensitive to differences among our population, but many of the entering students we see come from high schools where the curriculum might have been stiflingly sensitive in that teachers were not allowed to talk about certain pertinent issues in the lives of young people. For example, in North Carolina, where I taught high school, any conversation about sex was legally limited to discussions of abstinence. Especially among undergraduates, and freshmen especially among them, I've noticed that there is a reticence on the part of many students to talk about certain things—sexuality, gender, and race issues especially.

James "Bucky" Carter

In the freshman composition classes that I've been involved in, I've had to let the students know in every case that it was OK to talk about these issues, that it was acceptable to explore them in an open forum and even acceptable to disagree about topics within them. Though we certainly cannot blame educators at the secondary level for their reluctance to discuss certain things in their classrooms, we must be aware that at the college level we must inform students that it is acceptable to share different life experiences, methods of upbringing, and every other possible diversity. And we must allow them to feel it is safe to share their thoughts and views. Though we should be thankful that people seem more sensitive to others nowadays, we must also let our students know that college is a time when all thoughts are valid material, that the parachute works best when open. Of course, there are those who abuse this reminder, allowing their windbreakers to fill with a little too much air underneath them. These folks, I have to remind myself, have turned their parachutes into hot air balloons, and we all know what hot air balloons are full of.

This next reminder is both practical and ideological but, like any belief, is of little worth if not carried out. "Be a key ring, Bucky! Let them latch on you." I was the first member of my family to go to college. No one expected me to do anything like enter Western Carolina University in the fall of 1995. My family would have been happy to see me finish high school. Coming to college was an absolutely life-altering event for me, and if I hadn't been lucky enough to find people like Doctors John Habel, Denise Heinze, Gayle Miller, and Mary Warner, I don't know if I could have stood the brunt of the culture shock. Every day of my life, I try to keep in mind that I may be a scholar in the making, I may get paid to publish someday, but I am where I am to teach. *Teaching* is the one essential role of the university, even the research university. It's why universities exist. Students who can find someone to latch on to stand a better chance of getting involved, doing well, and finishing their programs than those who do not. It's proven fact. Be a mentor. Use your office hours for more than surfing the Web. Establish relationships that transcend four years. There are few things more rewarding than knowing your presence and support can help a person graduate. Think of how many people you assume have read your work. Now think of the number of students whose lives you have or could have touched. I'm absolutely positive the numbers are lopsided. Your peers may have read your articles and books and remembered the ideas but probably not your name. Those students you reach out to will remember you, and they can be your greatest legacy.

I hold this reminder close to my heart, and I hope that you will too. I know that some of you are reading this and thinking about the students who just wouldn't leave you alone, the ones who stopped by during every office hour and even tried to eat lunch with you—while you were already sitting with a colleague! Others of you are thinking about your own academic environment and know that you've accepted the standard perception that getting to know students just isn't professional. To you, I'm growling again, but this time I've no qualms about growling to your face (the rest of you can bask in my approval for a moment). I remind myself every day that I am where I am because of others' investment of time and hard work, and you are too.

Having just read my comments above, you might think I'm one of those new-wave liberal youngsters who just hasn't accepted the crashing wave of oppression that is professionalism. If so, you're right, and I hope I never do. College and university professors are a stodgy, conservative lot of coots, and, never having cared for the condition as a kindergartener, I hope I never fall prey to the inclination to be "cooty."

In fact, one of my other ideological reminders is, "Bucky, make your own definition of professionalism." This might be the most difficult to follow of all my suggestions to myself. Academic departments are rife with peer pressure, especially for those not yet at the associate level or tenured, and even we meager graduate students can see it when it rears its abominable head. But I've never known a teacher worth his or her salt at any level who didn't bend the rules or stretch one or two out to their breaking points. Now, I won't go so far as to advocate taking dangerous risks, but I will suggest that professors decide what "dangerous" means to them. At my current institution, especially, teachers are advised not to meet students at local coffee houses, restaurants, or anywhere outside of the office (and advised to keep the door open too); even the library is somewhat suspect. Certainly there are good reasons behind this line of thinking—we are in a sue-happy society, after all, and one or two perverse instructors here and there may have ruined such semisocial outings for the bulk of us, but I urge those collegiate teachers to decide on things like this for themselves. Some universities still think it uncouth to have a class outside on the lawn, even if a professor is studying *Leaves of Grass*! Learn your institution; get a good sense of what the unspoken no-nos are; then be your own person as much as you feel you can. I strive to do this in every aspect of my life, in fact, and I constantly remind myself to inculcate it into my teaching as well.

Oh, my weary-eyed friends—and we are friends now, right?—you've read this far, which means you have withstood possibly being called a coot, being accused of having a repressed sex drive that shows itself in your classroom gaze, and even having seen threatened many of the daily norms you may have become comfortable with. Surely you'd have left me by now if you didn't still

James "Bucky" Carter

like me, eh? I have but one reminder left. I am sure my stable of reminders will grow as I do, and the words of those around me will certainly have opened my eyes to many others I should incorporate, but please stick with me long enough to let me share this most important self-reminder: "Laugh at them; laugh at yourself, Bucky!"

If I were a doctor and had to write one prescription to university departments nationwide without knowledge of individual trends in particular departments, I'd probably prescribe a laxative. Unfortunately, I'm sure I'm not alone. Let's face it. Academics have a reputation for being stuffy to the point of being clogged, among students, among peers, among the general public. (You didn't think I'd stop teasing you in my last reminder, did you?)

I often remind myself to take time once a day, week, or month to "let it all out." I repeat to my tired mind, "Never take yourself so seriously that you can't laugh at your mistakes." I remember the time when I meant to say "part" but it came out "fart." I remember that there will always be times when I deal with an individual student in absolutely the most inappropriate manner, no matter how hard I try.

I am a teacher, but I am only human. I try to remember that and to remind my coworkers of it while I'm at it. "Reflect, mend, and laugh it off. And laugh at them too, the undergraduates because they are so clueless, the graduate students because they need the bran worse than you do." One of my favorite laughs came recently when a student in my English 102 class sent me an e-mail stating that, having finished his final draft at 2:00 A.M., he was so happy that he did a victory dance. While dancing, he says, his foot caught the cord to his computer and he ended up "busting a move" while at the same time busting his PC, inadvertently and magically, I might add, losing his paper forever. Yes, it was a lie. But it was a good lie. Good lies make me laugh. What's your favorite laughable excuse? Remember it. That one was so good I keep a copy of the e-mail folded in my wallet, just as a little reminder of what a very humorous position I am in as an educator.

Whether you are a beginning professor or at the end of a long career, if you are on faculty, you too were where these young people are now. Remember your youth through them; remember how dumb you were even when you were at your smartest. Your students are *so* laughable, and you'll need to be able to chuckle on bad days. Even if you take yourself seriously in class, don't be afraid to laugh at the students, yourself, your mistakes, and your triumphs. This is, indeed, one reminder that I'm sure I'll always be able to update, but one that I hope I never forget.

Now, that wasn't so hard to read, was it? I know as soon as you learned I was a student the innate urge to grab a pen and mark my awkward phrases overcame you, but you held back, and I'm proud of you for it. That's what teaching is all about anyway, right? Learning from and listening to each other? Acknowledging oneself as a life-long learner? I think it is, and again, I appreciate your time reading over my list of "notes to self," and I'm not just saying that. What? The backpack on my back that points me out as an insincere graduate student? Ignore it. Look, I've got this neat briefcase over here . . .

James "Bucky" Carter

Good at Any Age

D. Allen Carroll

The summer, with its lazy digression of three long months, is passing.[1] It's time for us in the English department to gather again—to greet old colleagues, welcome those new among us, make announcements, and generally dedicate ourselves anew to the cause we serve: English, the language and the various cultures that depend on it. This session, the only time all of us meet formally in the year, has a long tradition, though never before have there been quite so many of us. In the fall of 1940, which is as far back as anyone here can remember, we were seventeen. Of that seventeen, fifteen were full-time faculty and two were graduate assistants. Most of you today are young, very young, which was not the case then. The young now do most of our teaching. Young teachers, once they get a few years of experience, are the best. "That age is best which is the first," the poet says. You've all the magic energies of youth, the vitality; you teach with the most active intuition; and you know what's going on in the world of your students. What you teach in those lower-division courses will serve as the basic fabric of your own imaginative lives for the duration. If you would know a thing, teach it. All the literary allusions in Thomas Wolfe's *Look Homeward, Angel,* I have been told, all of them, including the title itself, came out of the sophomore survey of British literature that Wolfe taught at NYU (using the old Woods, Watt, and Anderson anthology). Yours can now be the glamour of being an English teacher—and there is such a thing—the exhilaration, the respect of your students, and, with all, the tedium, low pay, and alas, perhaps, the absence of state or institutional appreciation, which you hope to have, which you may or may not have.

It will be a little bumpy at first, for those new to it. One friend, years ago, facing thirty-five women students at what was then called "Woman's College" in Greensboro, in his first-ever teaching experience, looked out at them, as he described it to me, then down at the lectern, out at them again, and threw up. I notice that Arthur Schlesinger, the younger, in his memoir just out, recalls the same terror in his first teaching assignment at Radcliff. During his first few months, he regularly walked into the faculty restroom before class and threw up. Another friend, one who started out when I did, had a recurrent dream that his father appeared in his class and urinated all over the board. There are ways of reducing such fears early on. Ask students a few simple questions about the assignment for the day. You'll see how much you have to teach them. And go to the library; if it's *A Doll's House,* then read ten introductions in the school anthologies of our time. You'll be an expert.

I remember being so young as you, though not easily: "The old dog barks backward, without getting up, / I can remember when he was a pup." Or, to turn from Frost to Stoppard, I think of a charming wisp of a fantasy in a recent play, *The Invention of Love.* Stoppard sets up a meeting between the old Housman, now a spirit of the dead, and the young Housman, a student at Oxford. It's the old Housman who speaks the following: "Where can we [two] sit down before philosophy finds us out? I'm not as young as I was. Whereas you, of course, are."

There is always advice for the young, too much of it to go around, but very little for those of us on the other side of the curve, those whose numbers begin to tell, those careering downward, perhaps out of control, who become, or fear they will, people on whom one thing or another is lost.

The memory goes first, I'm told; and a good memory, Gilbert Highet says in *The Art of Teaching,* is one of three "absolutely essential" abilities of the good teacher. On a single day recently, I could not recall three names—in the morning, Iris Murdoch; in the afternoon, Christopher Wren; and in the evening, Nelson Algren. And there is enough data in the anecdotage of the profession to bring on anxiety attacks. John Livingston Lowes of Harvard, it has been said, in the autumn of his career would often give the same lecture twice in succession, or forget to give one at all, and he was an icon in our craft. One of our own colleagues, now a former colleague, managed on one occasion to cross the lectures between his two courses, mismatching them, thereby confusing and alarming both classes. And one can grow weary and bored with it all. A friend at Tuscaloosa recently retired because, as he told me, after teaching *The Great Gatsby* twenty-nine times he couldn't "bear to ever think of it again." Good teaching, another of our colleagues once insisted, has to do with the "glands." And, he exclaimed as he strode gracefully off into early retirement, "when the juices go, you go."

The age factor is always out there, going its own way, doing its own thing, in ourselves and in others we contemplate, even when we aren't fully conscious of it. (It's always out there—like, like . . . Terre Haute, Indiana.) We try to recognize and anticipate its tendencies, its small debilities and embarrassments, and go about minimizing them. Swift made such an attempt when he was, like you, quite young, in a list of "not to" resolutions that he labeled "When I come to be old." "Not to tell the same Story over and over to the same People," "Not to talk much, nor of myself," "Not to be over severe with young People, but give Allowances for their youthful follies and weakness." And so on. To which we

180

Good at Any Age

might well have added for him: "Not to go mad and become thereby known as the 'mad Dean of St. Patrick's.'"

Let me offer another list of such rules, this one designed for the aging teacher, in fact for one particular sexagenarian in the homestretch, reminders of certain elements of good teaching threatened by the encroachment of age—a few precepts to be addressed, as it were, to old Polonius himself. The tables turned.

Remember their names. Memorize them. It's a must. For those my age this wouldn't be too large a problem—but for the memory thing—because most of us address them, in the old style, by last names only. It's generational and a matter of personal style. In the early sixties I bought into the new mode and first-named them all. We became chummy. The consequence was that their work was careless and late. I quickly changed the address to Mr., Miss, and, later, Ms. And it was a wonder to behold how their work got better and came in on time. Your relationships with students should be impersonal. Now, at an age when it might be good for me to use a first name now and then, especially outside of class, I can't trust my memory. Besides, I'm of some old school that says you have to earn the right to use someone's first name. My response to telemarketers who first-name me—as I slam the phone down—is this: "My *friends* call me *Mr. Carroll!*" Housman was notorious at London University for not recognizing his students, for snubbing them, to their great irritation; and there was some defiant chutzpah in the apology of his farewell address (as recounted by Gilbert Highet): "If I had remembered all of your faces," so went his excuse, "I might have forgotten more important things." We ourselves know better: "students need to believe you care about them as individuals" (Highet).

Do not do "close readings," or many of them, that method we old fogies were taught in the early sixties, certainly not in the lower-division courses. Two types of ambiguity will do, not seven, and no more than one paradox per class meeting. Keep it simple, general, direct. I'm delighted to find the following set down in Jacques Barzun's *Teacher in America:* "the discussion of any class must be superficial. If you dive below the surface with your pupil, you drown him." Besides, that old method is absolutely voracious of time, which leads to another precept.

Have a plan—it's there in your syllabus—and unless under severe duress, stick to it. My old office mate at Wake Forest, where I once taught, spent half his Brit lit course on Chaucer's "General Prologue," so close were his readings. He never planned it that way; he couldn't stop himself. And my predecessor here, in his age, or dotage, never made it to the last three plays on his Shakespeare syllabus. "A good old man, sir, he will be talking" (*Much Ado*). Get on with it!

181

Besides, if you stick to the syllabus, then you won't have to remember, as you drive in to teach, where you left off last time: if it's the third day on *King Lear* (out of five), then it's the storm scene. Students get confused and anxious when the syllabus is unreliable.

Which means, to move on, give each assignment the time it deserves in the course and no more. Never, for example, give more than fifteen minutes to any one sonnet, even to one of your favorites. It's to do with the students' attention span, their need for variety, and not with your own pleasure. A proposal of one of our own colleagues might help here. It reflects an old grievance among us: "If we get no raise this year," he was wont to say, "then we'll have to stop teaching before we get to the sonnets' final couplet."

Try to know when and why you're repeating yourself. Then at least you can make some saving adjustment. Otherwise, nothing can be more embarrassing, more of a failing in old age. "Some of you," you say as you make eye contact with a student or two from a former class, "some of you have heard me on this topic already." Repetition, of course, is in the nature of teaching: "Remember," I say again and again, "the word *symbolic* [which is a word they worry about] simply means *suggestive*." Major problems here are catchphrases, phonic phrases, verbal ticks that we're apt to use unconsciously. One of our colleagues from another department, now retired, when he spoke publicly would use the method of point and then counterpoint. When he finished with point and was about to turn to counterpoint, you always knew exactly what would follow: "Having said that...." In your exasperation, you wanted to yell out some other choices. Try "That said"! What about "Even so"? Or, perhaps my favorite, "Be that as it may." Listen to what you actually say.

Put something on the syllabus that students can in fact read and have some chance of enjoying. Don't include some text because *you* like it, because *you* teach it well, because *you* have something to say about it, because *you* enjoy yourself while teaching it. At issue here for me is a course like English 201, the first half of the Brit lit survey, that old horse that brought many a teacher into the profession. Thirty years ago, it's my impression, students could make their way through the assignments; now they can't, at least average students can't. You want to put *Rape of the Lock* on the syllabus? Don't fool yourself. They can't read it. You'll need to explain every single line in class, as you will whatever Donne there is and whatever Milton. That course is now—in my judgment—unteachable; only *Beowulf* at the beginning, in translation, and *Gulliver* at the end are accessible to students, which is why I stopped teaching it. And I had hoped to teach the "General Prologue" in its own language as I rode off into the sunset. I'm disappointed, true; but it's *their* course, not *mine*.

And, last of all, in this lesson for myself: take heart! You still have your uses. Hardin Craig, whose Shakespeare text, as revised by Bevington, we assign here, taught all across the country until he was well into his nineties. Bain Stewart, a fine teacher here, now retired, assures me that his last five years were the best. Old teachers have a place in the mix. They give students a long perspective, one with shade and depth, something like the advantage children are said to have who grow up in homes that have both parents and grandparents. Old teachers certainly aren't taken in by fads, whatever the current "-ism," and they may indeed have earned some wisdom. Two cultures meet and mix, producing one that is much improved.

If "to teach is to learn twice," as the saying goes, this long process should eventually make some difference. We finally get it right. That old saying means, according to the interpretation Joseph Epstein favors, "that we are not ready for education, at any rate beyond the kind that leads to anything resembling wisdom, until we are sixty, or seventy, or beyond" *(A Line Out for a Walk)*.

Note

1. This essay was presented at the start of academic year 2001–2 to the teaching faculty and graduate students of the Department of English at the University of Tennessee, Knoxville.

D. Allen Carroll

Contributors

Marcus L. Ambrester earned his Ph.D. from Ohio University and is currently Associate Professor in the School of Communication Studies at the University of Tennessee where he cofounded UT's Conflict Resolution Program and studies conflict mediation and communication theory. Based in part on a seminar he cotaught called "Couples, Communication and Compatibility," Dr. Ambrester created and teaches the GARP method of interpersonal communication, which is designed to teach people in relationships how to work through problems and to resolve disputes.

Linda B. Arthur is Professor of Apparel Merchandising, Design and Textiles at Washington State University. Her research explores the intersection of gender, ethnicity, and ideology and the impact of these social locations on women's appearance. The article in this book was written as a result of her teaching at the University of Hawai'i. While there, she won the Carnegie Foundation and the Council for Advancement and Support of Education (CASE) Professor of the Year award for the state of Hawai'i.

Dave Berque is Associate Professor of Computer Science at DePauw University, where he has taught since 1992, and where he has held an endowed University Professorship in recognition of sustained excellence in professional accomplishment, teaching, and service. His research interests lie in the areas of human-computer interaction, computer-supported cooperative work, pen-based computing, instructional technology, and assistive technology for low-vision students. Dr. Berque was selected as the 1997 Carnegie Foundation/CASE United States Outstanding Professor of the Year for Baccalaureate Colleges. He is also a United States patent holder and an instructional technology consultant to Dy Know (www.dyknow.com).

JAMES BUCHANAN is the 1986 Nobel Prize Laureate in Economic Science. He is currently Advisory General Director of the Center for Study of Public Choice at George Mason University and Distinguished Professor Emeritus, George Mason University and Virginia Polytechnic Institute. Dr. Buchanan is best known for developing the "public choice theory" of economics, which changed the way economists analyze economic and political decision-making. His work opened the door for the examination of how politicians' self-interest and noneconomic forces affect government economic policy. Professor Buchanan got his start with a B.A. from Middle Tennessee State College in 1940, followed by an M.S. from the University of Tennessee in 1941. After graduating from the University of Chicago with a Ph.D. in 1948, he held teaching positions at the University of Virginia, UCLA, and the Virginia Polytechnic Institute. Among the many influential books he has written are *The Calculus of Consent* (1962) with Gordon Tullock; *Cost and Choice* (1969); *The Limits of Liberty* (1975); *Liberty, Market, and State* (1985); and his autobiography, *Better than Plowing* (1992). Most recently Liberty Fund, Inc. has published a series called *The Collected Works of James M. Buchanan.*

RICHARD D. BUCHER is Professor of Sociology at Baltimore City Community College in Baltimore, Maryland. His primary areas of study are diversity, race and ethnic relations, and education. Dr. Bucher has explored these subjects by creating and teaching a variety of courses dealing with diversity, working on national grants to infuse diversity into the curriculum, and presenting research at national and international conferences. At BCCC, he served as the first Director of the Institute for Intercultural Understanding, a nationally recognized diversity education program. He is the author of *Diversity Consciousness: Opening Our Minds to People, Cultures, and Opportunities* and was honored as the 2000 Maryland Professor of the Year by the Carnegie Foundation for the Advancement of Teaching and the Council for Advancement and Support of Education.

ORVILLE VERNON BURTON is Professor of History and Sociology at the University of Illinois and a Senior Research Scientist at the National Center for Supercomputing Applications, where he is Associate Director for Humanities and Social Sciences. Dr. Burton's research and teaching interests include the American South, especially race relations, family, community, politics, religion, and the intersection of humanities and social sciences. He is the author of more than one hundred articles and the author or editor of eight books. The Carnegie Foundation for the Advancement of Teaching and the Council for Advancement and Support of Education selected him as the nationwide 1999 U.S. Research and Doctoral University Professor of the Year. In 2004, he received the American Historical Association's Eugene Asher Distinguished Teaching Prize.

D. ALLEN CARROLL, a specialist in the English Literary Renaissance, has taught for thirty-five years at the University of Tennessee, Knoxville, where he holds the J. Douglas Bruce Chair in Literature. In 1989 he won a UT Distinguished Teaching Award, given campuswide, and in 2003 the Cunningham Teaching Award, given by the College of Arts and Sciences. In 2002, he stepped down as head of the Department of English after over ten years in that position. For many summers he directed his department's Drama in England course.

JAMES "BUCKY" CARTER is a doctoral student in English Education at the University of Virginia. He has taught high school English, served as the Academically and Intellectually Gifted Specialist at South Davie Middle School in his hometown of Mocksville, North Carolina, and instructed freshman and sophomore English classes on the community college and university level. He is a North Carolina Teaching Fellow and holds B.S.Ed. and M.A. degrees in English as well as a B.A. in art history. He has gained local recognition as an award-winning tutor and teacher throughout his career. While studying at the University of Tennessee (M.A., 2002), he earned the Alwin Thaler Editorial Assistantship, which allowed him to help solicit essays for this publication as well as affording him the opportunity to write his own. He reviews his "notes to self" contents before every new class and continues to grow his list of reminders.

LIBBY FALK JONES is Professor of English at Berea College, where she teaches courses in introductory and advanced writing, journalism, and creative writing. As Founding Director and currently Faculty Associate of Berea's Center for Learning, Teaching, Communication, and Research, she has led faculty development programs for new and continuing faculty and served as campus liaison to AAHE's Carnegie Academy for the Scholarship of Teaching and Learning program. Coeditor of *Feminism, Utopia, and Narrative* (University of Tennessee Press, 1990), she has published articles, book chapters, and poems on teaching, faculty development, feminist pedagogy, women's academic career paths, critical reasoning, writing assignments, and writing centers. She taught previously in the English department at the University of Tennessee, Knoxville, where she received the John C. Hodges Award for excellence in teaching.

MICHAEL FLACHMANN is Professor of English and Director of University Honors Programs at California State University, Bakersfield. He has written eight books—most recently *Beware the Cat: The First English Novel, Teaching Excellence, Shakespeare's Lovers,* and *Shakespeare's Women*—plus over fifty scholarly articles. He has also worked for many years in the world of professional theatre, serving as dramaturg for more than eighty Shakespeare productions at such prominent west coast theatres as the Utah and Oregon Shakespearean festivals, the La Jolla Playhouse, and California Institute of the Arts. In 1995 the Carnegie Foundation named him United States Professor of the Year for Masters Colleges and Universities. Dr. Flachmann also holds a fourth-degree black belt in Judo and has taught classes in the sport for the past thirty years.

LOUIS J. GROSS is Professor of Ecology and Evolutionary Biology and Mathematics and Director of The Institute for Environmental Modeling at the University of Tennessee, Knoxville. He completed a B.S. degree in Mathematics at Drexel University and a Ph.D. in Applied Mathematics at Cornell University and has been a faculty member at UT since 1979. His scientific research focuses on computational ecology and the application of quantitative approaches to problems such as Everglades restoration and conservation biology. He has been recognized by the National Science Foundation as an educational leader for his efforts to enhance the quantitative training of life science students. He served as Chair of the National Research Council Committee on Education in Biocomplexity Research and is currently President of the Society for Mathematical Biology.

MICHAEL HEBRON is PGA of America Master Professional; owner of the School for Learning Golf in New York, Florida, and North Carolina; and an international consultant on golf instruction. *Golf Magazine* and *Golf Digest* named him one of the fifty best golf instructors in America. His work in golf instruction has also been recognized with awards such as the PGA Horton Smith Trophy, PGA Teacher of the Year at the national and MET Section levels, and the Lindy Award for recognition of work with junior golfers. In addition, he is the author of four books, including *The Art and Zen of Learning Golf* and *Golf Swing Secrets and Lies.*

MARILYN KALLET holds the Hodges Chair for Distinguished Teaching in the English Department at the University of Tennessee. In 2000, she won the National Alumni Outstanding Teacher Award. Dr. Kallet is the author of eleven books, including *How to Get Heat Without Fire* (poetry), and coeditor with Judith Ortiz Cofer of *Sleeping with One Eye Open: Women Writers and the Art of Survival.* Recent poems have appeared in *New Letters, Prairie Schooner,* and *Tar River Poetry.* Dr. Kallet has won the Tennessee Arts Commission Literary Fellowship in Poetry and has been named Outstanding Woman in the Arts by the Knoxville YWCA. Her first children's book, *One for Each Night: Chanukah Tales and Recipes,* was published in 2003. Her new book of poems, *Circe, After Hours,* was published by BkMk Press, University of Missouri–Kansas City, in 2005.

MICHAEL L. KEENE is Professor of English at the University of Tennessee, where he created and is former director of the concentration in technical communication. He also teaches in the graduate program in rhetoric and composition. In addition to articles and chapters in numerous journals and books, his publications include ten books and two in progress, several with coauthor Kate Adams, such as *Research across the Disciplines* (Mayfield, 1999), *Instant Access* (McGraw-Hill, 2003), and a work in progress, *Alice Paul: American Gandhi*.

FATHER LEOPOLD KEFFLER, O.F.M. Conv., is Associate Professor of Biology at Marian College in Indianapolis, a Catholic college known for excellent teaching and learning in the Franciscan and liberal arts tradition. He holds bachelor's and master's degrees in religious sciences from the Assumption Seminary and College in Chaska, Minnesota, as well as a master's in combined sciences and a doctorate in biology from the University of Mississippi. He is a Franciscan friar in the Conventual tradition. Father Leopold is a self-described "academic vagabond." He accumulated his undergraduate and graduate courses at six different colleges and universities and has taught in four. He has taught more than fifteen courses over the years, including embryology, liturgy, and zoology—each of which was his favorite at the time he was teaching it.

CATHLEEN KENNEDY is the Director of Technology for the Berkeley Evaluation and Assessment Research Center at the University of California, Berkeley. Her research focuses on online learning and assessment, with an emphasis on using item response modeling to measure multiple aspects of learning. She is particularly interested in helping teachers and students understand interactions between learner readiness and teaching strategies. She earned her Ph.D. in quantitative methods in education from the University of California, Berkeley, where her dissertation was granted an Outstanding Doctoral Dissertation Award in 2001. Dr. Kennedy was a Carnegie Foundation U.S. Professor of the Year in 1998–99.

ROBERT LANGS, M.D., is a psychiatrist and psychoanalyst, and the author of 43 books and some 150 papers on psychotherapy, dreams, and the human condition. He is the creator of the Strong Adaptive or Communicative Approach, which focuses on the impact of unconscious perceptions of traumatic events and unconscious wisdom in emotional life, subjects he also explores through one- and two-act dramas. He is an Honorary Fellow at the School of Psychotherapy and Counselling, Regent's College, London.

DAVID LOUZECKY is a Professor of Philosophy at the University of Wisconsin College in Sheboygan, Wisconsin. He specializes in ethics and social philosophy and is the coauthor of *The Good Life: Personal and Public Choices*. Dr. Louzecky took his Ph.D. from the University of Wisconsin–Madison in 1975 and served as chair of the philosophy department of the thirteen campuses of UW Colleges from 1996 to 1999. The Carnegie Foundation and CASE named him Wisconsin Professor of the Year in 2000.

SRINIVASAN "RAJAN" MAHADEVAN received his first master's degree in psychology from Mysore University in India; his second came from Kansas State University. In 1999, Florida State University granted him the Ph.D. in psychology. Dr. Mahadevan traces his current interest in human memory back to the time when as a boy he memorized the license plate numbers of all the vehicles at a house party. From 1983 to 1987, he was listed in the *Guinness Book of World Records* for memorizing 31,811 digits of Pi. He is currently a lecturer in psychology at the University of Tennessee, where his teaching has been honored twice. In 2001, he won the Provost Teaching Award; in 2003, he was given the Kathryn White Davies Teaching Award for Psychology.

HELENA MEYER-KNAPP has been teaching Political and International Studies at The Evergreen State College for twenty years. Teachers there are encouraged to develop carefully considered pedagogy and are particularly committed to connecting theory with real-world experiences. Meyer-Knapp's research centers on peacemaking and specifically on the processes by which warring communities decide that the time has come to end their fighting. Her book, *Dangerous Peace-Making*, was published in 2003. Her work in this field has received support from the Carnegie Council on Ethics and International Affairs and from the Bunting Institute (now called the Radcliffe Institute for Advanced Study) at Harvard University.

APRIL MORGAN earned the Ph.D. in Government at Georgetown University. Currently she is Assistant Professor of Political Science at the University of Tennessee, where she specializes in intersections between international relations theory and international law. Dr. Morgan's research interests include the war on terrorism, state sovereignty, normative issues, and pedagogy. An NEH fellowship sparked *Ethics and Global Politics* (Kumarian Press, 2004), edited with Lucinda Joy Peach and Colette Mazzucelli. Her work in the classroom has been recognized by Georgetown University with the Edmund A. Walsh School of Foreign Service Honored Faculty teaching medal and by UT with the Chancellor's Award for Excellence in Teaching, as well as the National Alumni Association's Outstanding Professor of the Year Award.

PHYLLIS RAPHAEL is the author of a novel (*They Got What They Wanted*, Norton) and a short story collection, *(Beating the Love Affair Rap and Other Tales)*. Her fiction, essays, reviews and travel pieces have appeared in the *New York Times*, the *International Herald Tribune*, the *Village Voice*, *Vogue, Mirabella, Redbook, Harper's*, the *American Book Review, Boulevard*, and *Creative Nonfiction* and in the anthology *Seasons of Women* (Norton). She is the recipient of a PEN Syndicated Fiction Award and three Yaddo Fellowships. She is currently Associate Professor of Creative Writing at Columbia University. Her memoir of London in the 1960s will be published in 2005 by Riverhead Books of Putnam/Penguin.

GAYLE M. SEYMOUR received her Ph.D. in 1986 at the University of California, Santa Barbara, and is now Professor of Art History at the University of Central Arkansas. Her research areas include Pre-Raphaelite painting, contemporary public art, and women artists. She was the recipient of the 1993 UCA Teaching Excellence Award and in 1998 was the U.S. Master's University and Colleges Professor of the Year, awarded by the Carnegie Foundation and CASE.

JANE TOMPKINS earned her B.A. in English at Bryn Mawr College and her Ph.D. at Yale University. She has taught at a number of colleges and universities in the United States. She has published on literary theory, the opening of the American canon, popular culture, and women's writing. Initially she became known for her anthology *Reader Response Criticism: From Formalism to Post-Structuralism* (1980) and for *Sensational Designs: The Cultural Work of American Fiction, 1790–1860* (1985). In 1992 the American Popular Culture Association gave *West of Everything: The Inner Life of Westerns* the Ray and Pat Browne Award for Best Book on Popular Culture. Professor Tompkins has also been a leader in innovative pedagogy. In 1998, her memoir, *A Life in School: What the Teacher Learned* (Perseus Press, 1996) won the Frederic W. Ness Award for a book on liberal education granted by the American Association of Colleges and Universities. Currently, as Special Assistant to the Provost for the Campus Environment at the University of Illinois at Chicago, she creates lounge and café spaces and renovates classrooms as a way of making the university a friendlier environment.

ROBERT UNGER grew up near Nuernburg, Germany, where he earned national titles in both roller-skating and ice-skating before starring as a principal skater in Holiday on Ice and other European ice shows for eighteen years. During that time, he coached two German skating champions and a Ladies World champion (1954). In his early days at the Ice Chalet in Knoxville, Tennessee, he instituted

Contributors

for-credit university ice skating classes, helped pioneer the first recreational (amateur) competitions, and developed a test structure with eighteen levels and four types of skating for the Ice Skating Institute (ISI), now an international organization. He went on to earn the PSA Master's rating in figures, freestyle, administration, and group instruction. He has been a longtime board member of ISI, ISI Man of the Year, as well as judge and chief referee at numerous skating competitions. In 1983, he was inducted into the Ice Skating Hall of Fame and in 2000 won the ISI Lifetime Achievement Award.

DOROTHY WALLACE earned her B.S. from Yale University and her Ph.D. from the University of California at San Diego. Today, she is Professor of Mathematics at Dartmouth College. She has published more than fifty articles, books, and videos on matters such as Selberg's Trace Formula, norm-quadratic residue codes, numeracy, and the relationship between museum art and math. She has also served as principal investigator for an NSF grant to develop interdisciplinary courses involving faculty from all over campus. In 2000 she was named the New Hampshire Carnegie Foundation/CASE U.S. Professor of the Year. In addition to her research, she is currently involved with a variety of educational projects, including "The Electronic Bookshelf," an online publisher of curricular materials, and "Open Calculus," a free online calculus course.

JERRY WEINTZ is a professional artist who resides in East Tennessee. His extensive portfolio contains galleries devoted to several styles of art ranging from Egyptian to Victorian.

JACKIE WILCOX is Professor and Chair of the Department of English and Languages at Northeastern State University in Tahlequah, Oklahoma. Born in Winchester, England, the eldest of four girls, she grew up "naturally bossy"— "perfect teacher material" in her words. Dr. Wilcox spent fifteen years teaching in an English high school after graduating with a double major in French and linguistics. In her second life, she obtained a B.Ed. and M.A. in English from Western Illinois University and received the Delyte Morris Doctoral Fellowship from the University of Southern Illinois, where she completed the Ph.D. in English. Her particular area of interest today is the English novel. She is also a Carnegie Foundation/CASE Oklahoma Professor of the Year. She lives with her Kansan husband and a fat, egocentric golden retriever.

THOMAS W. WOOLLEY JR. is Professor of Statistics in the School of Business at Samford University and a Templeton Fellow participating in the Seminars in Science and Christianity at the University of Oxford. His primary areas of scholarly interest include the fundamental nature of chance, the interface of chance and Christian theology, outlier detection methodology, Bayesian analysis, statistical education, and statistical and quantitative literacy. In 2000, he was Carnegie Foundation/CASE Alabama Professor of the Year. Since 1981, he has authored more than sixty publications.

Index

Cold War, 147–48

collaboration: in evaluations of teachers, 101; learning, effectiveness of, 113; learning, as a strategy for teaching, 8, 95, 146, 172; learning, as a theme, xx; and team teaching, 163

competition: in grading, 146; in hierarchies 14–15; and technical skills, 61

confidentiality, 36

confusion: and learning, 125–26; and student interaction, 182

Cousteau, Jacques, 97

Craig, Hardin, 183

culture: material, 151–55; social, xxi, 69, 145, 151–54, 183

cultural baggage, 137–38

D

Dark Star Park (Holt), 94

D'Avanzo, Charlene, xxii

Davis, Franky, 135

Dead Poets Society, 60

Decoding Your Dreams (Langs), 32

dichotomous thinking and race, 131–32

Dickinson, Emily, 52–53

diversity: consciousness of in teaching, xii, 137–40; cultural, 151; gender-based, 148

Diversity Consciousness: Opening Our Minds to People, Cultures, and Opportunities (Bucher), 139

Donne, John, 48

"do no harm," xviii, 22, 25

Dorra, Henri, 93, 96

dreams: *Class Dream* (Jones), 55; *Decoding Your Dreams* (Langs), 32; and perceptions, 32–40; in poetry, 27–28; and psychoanalysis, 32–40

drugs: and boundaries, 28; student experiences, 120

E

education: and aging, 183; and citizenship, 9; defined, 49; expectations, 3–4; as life training, 10, 77; and the university, 77

encoded perception, 33–35

End of Education, The (Postman), 157

Essential Elements, 95

F

facts: acquisition, 126; and analysis, 133; the analysis of, concerning gender, 143; and teaching in correctional facilities, 159

fear: and diversity, 138; and moral freedom, 82–83; of peer evaluation, 173; of public speaking, xi; in students, 75–77; and teaching, 7, 27, 59, 71–72, 169–70, 179–80

feminism, 143–49

Finite and Infinite Games (Carse), 3–4, 10

First Principle of Golf, The, 70

flow state of learning, xii, xix, 72–73

food: role in building relationships, 27, 42

frame breaks: in student/teacher relationships, 34, 38–40

frame exercises, 32, 36

G

gender: biases, 173; and class/race relations in education, 132; and cultural baggage, 137–38; and feminism, 143–49

Ghosts of Diophantus (Harper), 126

Gilchrist, Matt, 27

M

Making of Knowledge in Composition, The (North), 54

mastery: as an instructor, 45; of a subject, 7

mathematics: and critical thinking, 119–21; the teaching of, 123–27

memory: and aging, 180–82; of college, 75

memorization: and mastery, 7–8; and regurgitation, 15; and teaching, 59

Mind of the South (Cash), 135

Minnich, Elizabeth, 144

Minutemen and Their World, The (R. Gross), 133

mistakes: pedagogical, 45, 144; and recovery, 158, 176; while teaching, 103

Mohanty, Chandra, 143

N

nontransference, 31

notes: and study habits, 4, 157; *Note to Self* (Carter), 167–77; in use in teaching, 117

O

Oh! Pascal! (Cooper), 101–2

online courses, 9

overteaching, 19–23, 66–67

P

Palmer, Parker, 54

pedagogical strategies, evaluation of, 28, 47, 49, 52, 60–62, 66, 71, 85–92, 101, 106–7, 109–15, 117, 124–26, 152–55, 173, 181–82

Pedagogy of the Oppressed (Freire), xx, xxii, 126

perfection: as the enemy of good, xii, 25; and overcoming obstacles, 119; and practice, 6

performance anxiety, 62

Perkins, Maxwell, 21

Perls, Frederick, 13

philosophy: in pedagogical strategies, 157–65

physical contact: as a positive influence, 41–42; and student boundaries, 28, 37, 61

play: as a learning tool, 25, 39, 60, 73

Politics of Experience, The (Laing) 16

PowerPoint: and technology, 171–72; use in lecturing, 109–11

Power T seating configuration, 169

practice: and body memory, 65–66; to improve teaching methods, 45; student perceptions of, 61

practitioner lore, xv; and Stephen North, 54

problem-solving: and critical thinking, 121; and golf, 70; and problem-based learning, 98

professionalism, 175

proper instructional level, 46

psychotherapy: uses in pedagogy, 31–40

R

race: and classroom dynamics, xxi, 27, 131–35; and dichotomous thinking, 131–32; and diversity issues, 137–41; and resistance, 173

Red Cross, 85, 90

repetition: in learning, 121; in teaching, 65, 111–12, 182; repetitive nature of teaching, 46

respect: students to teacher, 81–82, 117; teacher to students, 5, 60, 160–61; mutual, 98, 152, 164 review sessions, 114

Rhetoric of Motives, A (Burke), 14–15

Ripa, Cesare: on painting, 93

Robinson, Jon, 61

Rogers, Thomas, 51–52

Ruddick, Sarah, 143

S

Schlesinger, Arthur, 179

selective ignorance, 121

Self-Portrait as the Allegory of Painting (Gentileschi), 93

September 11, 2001: impact on pedagogy, 154

sex: and classroom gaze, 175; and clerical scandal, 42; disrespect of sex symbols, 81; and frame exercises, 37–38; and psychotherapy, 33; as a writing topic, 22

Shaw, Irwin, 20

Save Outdoor Sculpture project (Smithsonian), 94

socio-economics: impact on education, xxi, 132–33, 137–40

Socrates: philosophical tradition, 157; and student perceptions, 76

Socratic method, 162–63

Song for the Class (Jones), 56

"spoon-feeding," 111

Stafford, William: on vision, 91–92; and writer's block, 25

Staver, John R., xxii

stereotypes: pedagogical strategies for coping, 137; and race, 135; of teachers, 4–5

Stewart, Bain, 183

stress-point learning, xix, 71–72

study habits, 8–9

surprise: and lesson plans, 83; teaching and parenting, 31; and team teaching, 145; when teaching, 3–10

syllabus: coverage, 161; defined, xii, 110; flexibility, 119, 158; struggles, 101–2; values, 144, 154–55, 181–82

T

Tao Te Ching, 87

Teacher in America (Barzun), 181

teaching: authority, xx, 52–53, 81–82, 117, 133, 160, 168–69; from behind, 85–92; defined, 16–17, 31, 61, 81, 109, 124; ideal frame, 36–37; practice, 117; syndromes, xii, 83; team, 90, 145

Teaching to Transgress (hooks), xxii, 126

Theory of Computation, 107

Theory of Justice, A (Rawls), 162

Titus Andronicus, 48

trained incapacity to learn, 15, 69

transference, 31, 34

Transforming Knowledge (Minnich), 143, 147

trigger decoding, 35

truth: and feminist pedagogy, 147; and how-to instruction, 70; and knowledge, 48; personal, 46; and psychotherapy, 33–34; about students, 81

Twain, Mark, 123

U

Untaught Teacher, The (Levertov), 22–23

Uptaught (Macrorie), xvii, xxii

Utah Shakespearean Festival, 46–47

V

valid unconscious perceptions, 31

Vulnerable Teacher, A (Macrorie), 89

The Art of College Teaching was designed and typeset on a Macintosh computer system using QuarkXPress software. The body text is set in 10/13 Minion and display type is set in DaddyOHip. This book was designed and typeset by Kelly Gray and manufactured by Thomson-Shore, Inc.